# GOLD! GOLD! GOLD! GOLD!

## Sixty-Eight Rich Men on the Steamer Portland.

## STACKS OF YELLOW METAL!

### Some Have $5,000, Many Have More, and a Few Bring Out $100,000 Each.

## THE STEAMER CARRIES $700,000.

### Special Tug Chartered by the Post-Intelligencer to Get the News.

# CALL OF THE KLONDIKE

## A TRUE GOLD RUSH
## ADVENTURE

**DAVID MEISSNER** and **KIM RICHARDSON**

CALKINS CREEK
AN IMPRINT OF HIGHLIGHTS
Honesdale, Pennsylvania

# I WANTED the gold,

# and I sought it;

I scrabbled and mucked like a slave.

Was it famine or scurvy—I fought it;

I hurled my youth into a grave.

I wanted the gold, and I got it—

Came out with a fortune last fall,—

Yet somehow life's not what I thought it,

And somehow the gold isn't all.

—Robert Service, Klondike poet

1874–1958

Stanley Pearce

Stanley Pearce and Marshall Bond were friends, business partners, and graduates of Yale University. Both had mining backgrounds and happened to be in the right place at the right time in the summer of 1897. They had been on a prospecting trip to Vancouver Island and returned to Seattle the night before the S.S. *Portland* docked. When they started their Klondike expedition, Pearce was twenty-six years old and Bond was twenty-nine.

When Stanley Pearce was two years old, his father, Richard Pearce, moved the family from England to Colorado to manage a mining operation. Richard Pearce was a talented metallurgist who constantly sought out new mining opportunities. Throughout their youth, Stanley and his three brothers traveled widely in Canada, the United States, and Latin America to look after their father's mining interests. Even though Stanley spent much of his life in the U.S., he always identified with his British roots.

# Adventurers

Marshall Bond

Marshall Bond's father was a prominent judge and a risk-taking businessman who moved his family often as he followed mining and business opportunities around the United States. As a result, Marshall grew up hunting, fishing, driving cattle, and exploring many parts of the western United States. After graduating from Yale in 1888, Marshall moved to Seattle, where he worked for his father's mining company and started his own real estate business.

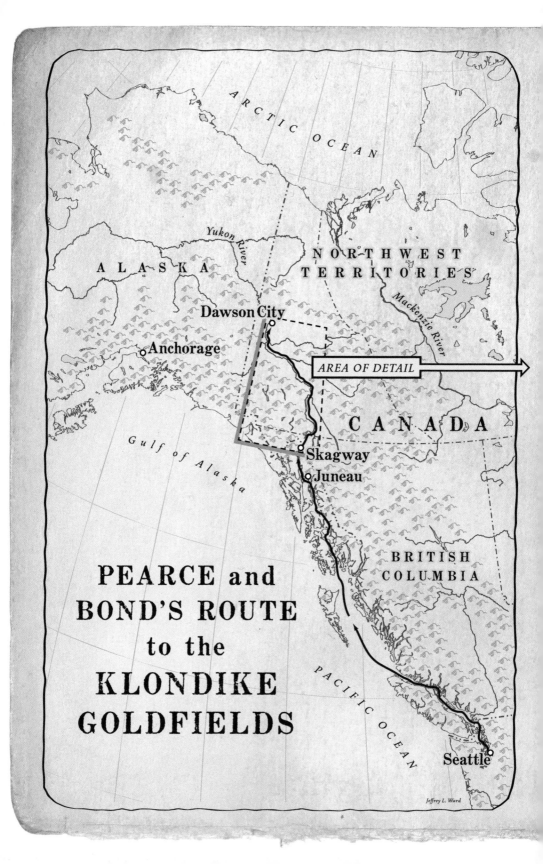

ARCTIC OCEAN

Yukon River

ALASKA

NORTHWEST TERRITORIES

Mackenzie River

Dawson City

Anchorage

AREA OF DETAIL

CANADA

Gulf of Alaska

Skagway

Juneau

BRITISH COLUMBIA

PEARCE and BOND'S ROUTE to the KLONDIKE GOLDFIELDS

PACIFIC OCEAN

Seattle

Jeffrey L. Ward

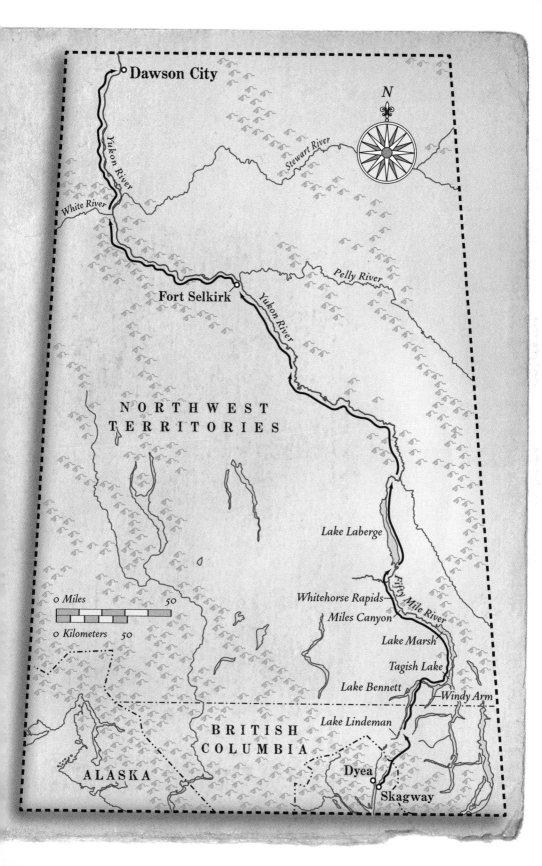

# CALL OF
# KLO

# THE
# NDIKE

GOLD STRI

Stores like Cooper & Levy sold tons of goods to eager stampeders.

# FEVER
# KES

We caught the fever and decided to go. Everybody seemed to be catching it.

—MARSHALL BOND

tanley Pearce and Marshall Bond were in Seattle, Washington, when it happened. On July 17, 1897, sixty-eight rugged miners stepped off the S.S. *Portland* steamship and made their way through the excited crowd. They were carrying large sacks filled with the most precious metal in the world—gold.

Stanley Pearce described the scene this way: "Thousands of people in the public square watched the weather-beaten and hardy adventurers stagger into the express office with sacks of gold, gold in blankets, in oil cans, and even in moccasins."

Together, these miners brought back an astounding four thousand pounds of gold. It was worth nearly one million dollars, which, by today's standards, would be many times that amount. Three days earlier, miners on another ship, the S.S. *Excelsior*, had arrived in San Francisco with large quantities of gold as well. Both groups of miners had found their gold in the same place: the Klondike region of northern Canada. Soon these discoveries would make headlines around the world.

In a matter of hours, many Seattle residents began planning their own trips to the goldfields. At a time when many Americans were either out of work or earning low wages, the prospect of striking it rich proved irresistible. Firemen, doctors, lawyers, ministers—and even the mayor of Seattle—quit their jobs and joined the rush.

"By the afternoon," Pearce wrote, "every man who could raise the necessary funds for a year's grub stake was rushing to the grocers, hardware merchants and clothiers to get together the necessary outfit to start by the next boat for the promised land, where the dreams of all should be realized."

In all of their excitement, eager prospectors underestimated the fact that the new goldfields were located more than 1,500 miles

# A YUKON OUTFIT.

8 Sacks Flour
150 lbs. Bacon
150 lbs. Split Peas
100 lbs. Beans
25 lbs. Evaporated Apples
25 lbs. Evaporated Peaches
25 lbs. Apricots
25 lbs. Butter
100 lbs. Granulated Sugar
1½ doz. Condensed Milk
15 lbs. Coffee.
10 lbs. Tea.
1 lb. Pepper
10 lbs. Salt
8 lbs. Baking Powder
40 lbs. Rolled Oats or Oatmeal
2 doz. Yeast Cakes
½ doz. 4 oz. Beef Extract
5 bars Castile Soap
6 bars Tar Soap
1 tin Matches
1 gal. Vinegar
1 box Candles
25 lbs. Evaporated Potatoes
25 lbs. Rice
25 Canvas Sacks
1 Wash Basin
1 Medicine Chest
1 Rubber Sheet
1 set Pack Straps
1 Pick
1 Handle
1 Drift Pick
1 Handle
1 Shovel
1 Gold Pan
1 Axe
1 Whip Saw

1 Hand Saw
1 Jack Plane
1 Brace
4 Bits, assorted, 3/16 to 1 in.
1 8-in. Mill File
1 6-in Mill File
1 Broad Hatchet
1 2-qt. Galv'd Coffee Pot
1 Fry Pan
1 Package Rivets
1 Draw Knife
3 Cov'd Pails, 4, 6, 8-qt. Granite
1 Pie Plate
1 Knife and Fork
1 Granite Cup
1 each Tea and Table Spoon
1 14-in. Granite Spoon
1 Tape Measure
1 1½-in. Chisel
10 lbs. Oakum
10 lbs. Pitch
5 lbs. 20d. Nails
5 lbs. 10d. Nails.
6 lbs. 6d. Nails.
200 feet ⅝ in. Rope.
1 Single Block
1 Solder Outfit
1 Pair Rowlocks
1 14-qt. Galvanized Pail
1 Granite Saucepan
3 lbs. Candle Wick
1 Compass
1 Candle Stick
6 Towels
1 Axe Handle
1 Axe Stone
1 Emery Stone

**Some of the foregoing articles are omitted by some miners.
Dealers will advise in all cases.**

Unsure of what they might be able to purchase up in Alaska and Canada, many stampeders brought more than a year's worth of supplies, similar to the list above.

north of Seattle, not far from the Arctic Circle. Dawson City, in Canada, the boomtown at the center of the gold rush, was so far north that on winter days the sun barely rose and temperatures could dip well below -60° F.

The journey there would be long and arduous, as gold seekers would soon find out. To reach Dawson City, most stampeders would travel by steamship to Alaska, haul gear over steep mountain passes into Canada, and then travel more than five hundred miles by boat down a series of lakes and rivers.

Most stampeders left for the Klondike from Seattle, which quickly transformed from an economically depressed city into a bustling port. Prospectors swooped into stores and bought thousands of dollars' worth of goods. Every store seemed to advertise Klondike gold rush supplies, whether it was boots, guns, sleds, beans, or "special" Klondike underwear. Some Seattle entrepreneurs even advertised regular dogs as sled dogs that could pull heavy loads across snowfields and up frozen rivers.

Within hours of seeing the gold, Stanley Pearce and Marshall Bond decided to mount their own Klondike expedition. Bond's father, who happened to be in Seattle at the time, agreed to fund part of it. Now all they needed was for Pearce's father to do the same. That morning, Pearce sent the following telegram to his father in Denver:

**WESTERN UNION TELEGRAM**
July 17, 1897, 9:15 a.m.
Seattle, Washington
To Richard Pearce:
News of wonderful richness of Klondyke northwest territory gold fields. Million dollars brought in last steamer. Excitement

here similar California forty nine. Believe it chances for me thirty days trip from here. Last steamer Tuesday. Two thousand capital needed. Gone one year. Answer at once if you favor or not.

Stanley Pearce

Marshall Bond also contacted Stanley's father:

**WESTERN UNION TELEGRAM**

July 17, 1897, 9:10 a.m.

Seattle, Washington

To Richard Pearce:

I think beyond question Klondyke diggings the grand opportunity. Forty five miners, just brought out million in dust. Many friends and prominent people here going. Reasonable, accessible and no hardships a man need fear.

My father here and advises going. Hope you will favor it. Can make monetary arrangements here for Stanley. Absent one year if worst happens, wages fifteen dollars a day and board.

Marshall Bond

## MARSHALL BOND DIARY

JULY 17, 1897

Steamer Portland arrived in early morning hours with 68 miners and over a million. The town went crazy when they saw these fellows carry their huge sacks into the Express office. It was the proof. . . . Everybody who can get away is going and the excitement is intense.

Response from Richard Pearce to his son Stanley:
"Wired you Seattle last night to draw . . . two thousand . . ."

# MARSHALL BOND DIARY

July 19, 1897.

Pearce received word from his father to draw for $2000. and go. Excitement at a fever heat. We were on the rush all day ordering our outfit. Wired to Butte to get a good miner.

July 20, 1897.

The excitement grows. Everyone going. Merchants beside themselves. My brother wired that he was coming. Engaged passage for him on S.S. Mexico, which sails the 25th.

July 22, 1897.

Bought three pack horses and arranged for their shipment on the Mexico, the 25th. Also bought two big dogs. Late in the afternoon outfit completed and put on board the ship.

Most stampeders needed time to get to Seattle from other parts of the country, buy supplies, assemble a team, and book passage on a ship heading north. This sometimes took months. Yet in less than one week, Stanley Pearce and Marshall Bond had already organized their expedition and bought tickets for the S.S. *Queen*, the first steamship headed for Alaska since the dramatic arrival of the S.S. *Portland*.

When Bond's brother, Louis, heard the news, he wanted to go, too. Louis quit his job on the family ranch in California, packed his bags, and prepared to travel on the S.S. *Mexico*, a steamship that would leave for Alaska just two days after the S.S. *Queen*.

# WHY

For thousands of years, humans have recognized gold as a rare, beautiful, and precious metal with unique properties. Gold is so durable that it is nearly indestructible. It is so malleable that it can be reshaped and used for many purposes. It is also soft enough that it can be combined with other metals, such as silver and copper. Over time, gold has been used to make jewelry as well

# GOLD?

as decorative objects, electrical circuitry, tooth fillings, coins, and more.

People have also seen gold as a good investment that generally keeps its value over time. In the 1870s, the United States adopted the gold standard, which linked the country's currency to gold. This meant that anyone could exchange gold for dollars at a set rate of exchange.

# RACE KLON D

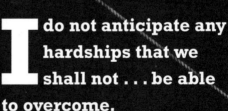

**I** do not anticipate any hardships that we shall not . . . be able to overcome.

—Marshall Bond

# TO THE
# IKE

When ships departed for Alaska, families, friends, and curious onlookers crowded the port to wish stampeders well.

## SILVER GOES LOWER THAN EVER

### A Drop of Half a Cent in the Price Recorded Yesterday in New York.

NEW YORK, July 27.—Silver was lower to-day than ever before. Until the decline of recent date the lowest prices were those of March 3 and 5, 1894, at the time of the closing of the Indian mints. The opening quotations to-day were bar silver 58¼, Mexican dollars 45¾, and the closing was 58¼ and 45¾, respectively. The local dealers can assign no other reason than lack of demand. There being no special orders of silver for any European country for mintage and India not being in the market, they regard the fall as natural.

The Evening Post's London financial cablegram to-day has the following:

"The fall in silver is exciting much interest. The impulse seems to come mainly from American selling, but the flatness of the Chinese exchange exceeds the extent warranted by the fall in silver. It is believed heavy interest payments by China abroad partly accounts for it. I understand that the negotiations are proceeding for a further issue of the Chinese loan of £16,000,000, but apparently nothing definite is done yet."

The total amount of silver shipped to Europe to-day was 712,000 ounces.

### SILVER QUESTION IN MEXICO.

### The Fall in the Price Interferes With Business Calculations.

CITY OF MEXICO, July 27.—The drop in silver announced to-day created much comment here in financial and business circles. The exchange on New York rose to 1.18 and even on the street to 1.10, and London exchange was quoted at 22 pence. If silver remains down, the loss to corporations having gold interest to meet abroad will be large and at the present basis gold interest on government loans abroad will require a million dollars more in silver per annum. Many orders for goods abroad have been canceled, merchants desiring to see how the exchange is going. It is generally believed that the sudden fall in silver is due to the unloading by large bullion holders, coupled with new gold discoveries and the continued small demand in India for silver. The fluctuation in exchange does more harm than low prices, as it makes impossible all calculations. The continued low prices, as it makes impossible all calculations. The continued low price of silver will revive the talk of adopting the gold standard, which would be ruinous to the new manufacturing industries. Bankers, while anticipating even lower prices for silver, believe there will be a reaction to a price which will permit something like steadiness in exchange and stability in business operations.

## HE'S OFF FOR THE KLONDYKE

### Stanley Pearce of Denver on the First Steamer to Go North.

### He Will Keep "The Republican's" Readers Thoroughly Posted.

### An Expert Mining Engineer as Well as a Fact Gleaner and Versatile Writer.

### With Complete Outfit and Traveling Companion, He's a Week Ahead of Other Correspondents.

Stanley B. Pearce, the mining engineer of Denver, was in Seattle en route to new mining camps in British Columbia, when the reports of the wonderful gold fields at Klondyke first reached Pacific coast points. Thereupon he decided to push out for Alaska as one of the advance guard of the fortune-seekers, with Klondyke as the objective point. While outfitting, prior to leaving by the first steamer, arrangements were made by telegraph between Mr. Pearce and The Republican by which Mr. Pearce is to act as correspondent for this paper during his journey to and stay in Klondyke. He fortunately has a week's start of other correspondents, and being an accepted authority on mining subjects, as well as a versatile writer, Republican readers may be assured of getting the first and reliable news from the new Eldorado. His first letter, necessarily short, follows:

ON BOARD STEAMSHIP QUEEN,

ESDAY MORNING, JULY 28, 1897.

# CAPT. RAY GOES TO THE YUKON

## He Is Detailed to Establish a Military Post in Alaska.

## Ordered to Report at Seattle Ready to Sail by August 5.

### He Will Take a Company of About Sixty-Six Men With Him.

### Capt. Ray Has a Notable Record, Having Spent Several Years in Alaska.

CHEYENNE, Wyo., July 27.—(Special.)—Captain Patrick Henry Ray, Eighth United States infantry, stationed here, received telegraphic notice to-day from the secretary of war that he had been detailed to command an expedition to the Yukon district, Alaska, for the establishment of a government post. Captain Ray's command will consist of a company of 63 men, two surgeons and two lieutenants. He is ordered to be at Seattle not later than August 5th and will proceed by steamer from that place to Michaelofski, about 100 miles north of the mouth

## DARING ROBBERY AT FLORENCE

### Jeweler Cloud Bound and Gagged in His Room and His Trunk Looted.

FLORENCE, Colo., July 27.—(Special.)—Between 10 and 11 o'clock last night I. T. Cloud was gagged and robbed in his own room. Mr. Cloud is a jeweler and kept some gold watches and cash in his room locked up in his trunk. Upon going to his

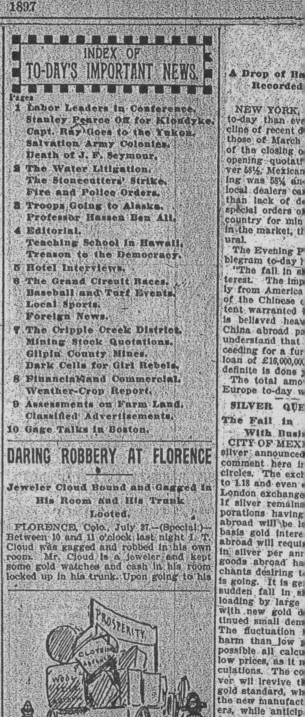

A Drop of Ha...
Recorded...

NEW YORK,
to-day than eve
cline of recent d
those of March
of the closing o
opening quotati
ver 58½. Mexican
ing was 58½ an
local dealers ca
than lack of d
special orders of
country for min
in the market, th
ural.

The Evening P
blegram to-day h
"The fall in si
terest. The imp
ly from America
of the Chinese c
tent warranted t
is believed heavy
China abroad pa
understand that
ceeding for a fur
loan of £16,000,00
definite is done y
The total amo
Europe to-day w

### SILVER QUE
The Fall in
  With Busi
CITY OF MEXI
silver announced
comment here in
circles. The exch
to 1.18 and even
London exchange
If silver remains
porations having
abroad will be la
basis gold intere
abroad will requi
in silver per ann
goods abroad ha
chants desiring t
is going. It is ge
sudden fall in si
loading by large
with new gold d
tinued small dem
The fluctuation i
harm than low p
possible all calcu
low prices, as it h
culations. The co
ver will revive th
gold standard, wh
the new manufac
ers, while anticip
for silver, believe
to a price that wi
steadiness in exc
business operation
tors and brakeme

By the time their ship was ready to depart, Pearce and Bond had gathered more than six thousand pounds of supplies and packed it all in fifty-pound canvas sacks. Their outfit included picks, axes, gold pans, rubber boots, rain jackets, sleeping bags, and even $100 lynx- and wolf-skin robes.

They had also hired three men to join their expedition: Bailey, Wickman, and Moore. One was a miner from Butte, Montana, and two were ex-policemen from Seattle.

Stanley Pearce described their early morning departure this way: "Several thousand people were at the dock to see the steamer depart, and some of the scenes were most affecting. All classes and conditions of men have joined the stampede—lawyers, merchants, doctors, prospectors."

---

## ON BOARD ALASKA EXCURSION STEAMSHIP QUEEN. JULY 23RD, 1897

Dearest Mother

I left the wharf unhappy as I had not written you. I meant to send you the last information but have been worked to death. Up all night for three nights. Have a man from Butte and two others. Outfit and grub largest & best from Seattle. Horses—dogs. (Underclothes thick and plenty) . . .

We are in fine shape for a fortune.

Dearest love to you Mother—the same to Father . . .

Goodbye—will send you word when I can.

Stanley Pearce

Ask father to pay all bills for me and keep account. Don't either of you worry as we are well equipped—

# THE DENVER REPUBLICAN

Denver, Colorado, Wednesday Morning, July 28, 1897

## HE'S OFF FOR THE KLONDYKE

--------

### Stanley Pearce of Denver on the
### First Steamer to Go North.

--------

### He Will Keep "The Republican's" Readers
### Thoroughly Posted.

--------

### An Expert Mining Engineer
### as Well as a Fact Gleaner
### and Versatile Writer.

--------

### With Complete Outfit and Traveling Companion,
### He's a Week Ahead of Other Correspondents.

--------

Stanley H. Pearce, the mining engineer of Denver, was in Seattle en route to new mining camps in British Columbia, when the reports of the wonderful gold fields at Klondyke first reached Pacific coast points. Thereupon he decided to push out for Alaska as one of the advance guard of the fortune-seekers, with Klondyke as the objective point. While outfitting, prior to leaving by the first steamer, arrangements were made by telegraph between Mr. Pearce and The Republican by which Mr. Pearce is to act as correspondent for this paper during his journey to and stay in Klondyke. He fortunately has a week's start of other correspondents, and being an accepted authority on mining subjects, as well as a versatile writer, Republican readers may be assured of getting the first and reliable news from the new Eldorado. . . .

For four days, Pearce and Bond traveled north
by steamship, past steep mountains, dense forests,
and dramatic glaciers.

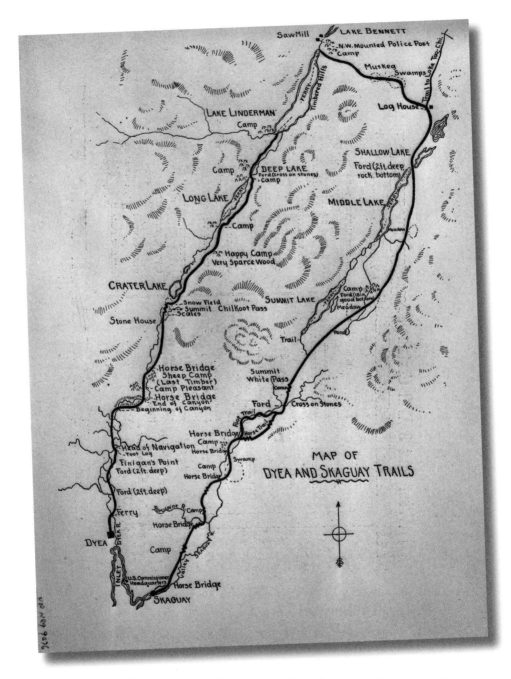

Stampeders could travel up the White Pass Trail from Skagway to the east or follow the Chilkoot Trail from Dyea. The two trails joined near Lake Bennett. This map was published in 1898, the year after Pearce and Bond made their trip.

On their way to Dawson City, most stampeders had two options for crossing Alaska's formidable Coast Mountains: the Chilkoot Trail and the White Pass Trail. Both routes had their advantages and disadvantages. The Chilkoot was very steep in places, but it was shorter, well established, and had Indian packers available for hire. The White Pass Trail was not as steep, but it was longer and there was no reliable word on the condition of the trail, including whether it had even been completed to the top of the pass.

To take the Chilkoot Trail, Pearce and Bond would need to land at the small town of Dyea, Alaska. To travel over the White Pass Trail, they would need to dock at the nearby port of Skagway. After much discussion, Pearce and Bond decided to land at Dyea and take the Chilkoot.

---

## On Board
## Alaska Excursion Steamship Queen.
## July 26, 1897

Dear Mrs. Pearce:—

We are running up a most beautiful sound somewhat wider than the Hudson river with huge snow-capped mountains rising almost straight up from the waters edge. Several large glaciers are in sight and the scenery beggars description. We have had our last civilized meal and within . . . an hour shall be at Dyea, our landing place.

Stanley and I hit it off well together, and tho' our trip promises to be a very trying one, I have no doubts we shall get on well together.

From Dyea, with the help of Indians, we shall pack our outfit over the mountains on our backs, put together our three boats (wh[ich] have already been made and taken apart) on Lake Lindeman, and then, excepting three portages of half a mile or so each, we should have plain sailing (or rather rowing) down the Yukon....

As to food and clothing—I really believe we have the best equipment that ever went into the Yukon.

I do not anticipate any hardships that we shall not only be able to overcome, but wh[ich] will be of great benefit to us physically.... The Capt. is going to lower our canoe first and thereby enable us to get ashore & bid for packers before the others can land, and as I must be looking after it, I shall have to close.

With kindest regards for yourself and Mr. Pearce, I am,

Sincerely Yours,

Marshall Bond

## MARSHALL BOND DIARY

July 26, 1897.

Arrived off Dyea about noon. Sea running high. Couldn't land on the rocks. Capt. Carroll went to Skagway in the launch and brought back word that the trail over White Pass was completed and pack horses in readiness. As we couldn't land at Dyea, and the reports bro[ugh]t by Carroll so favorable, all decided to go to Skagway.

We tied up at a little dock and worked most of the night unloading our stuff onto it.

The S.S. *Queen* unloads stampeders' supplies onto smaller boats to take to shore.

# THE DENVER REPUBLICAN

Bond and I, with a hundred others, were literally dumped here [in Skagway] . . . by Capt. Carrol of the Queen, and after almost superhuman efforts, working for 36 hours without food or sleep, we managed to collect our belongings. . . .

Too much criticism cannot be made of the treatment given the miners and other gold-seekers by the captains of the Queen and Mexico. They could not have treated cattle worse in food and accommodations, and as for their treatment of us in the discharge of our cargo, scattering it along the beach at low tide, where we had to fight day and night to save it, it was simply disgraceful. . . .

—Stanley Pearce

When Pearce and Bond landed at Skagway, it wasn't even a town. Bond noted that it basically consisted of a dock and a boarding house. Within weeks, Skagway would grow into a tent city and within months it would become a bustling town.

After scrambling to secure their supplies and set up camp, Pearce and Bond were dismayed to learn that the White Pass Trail, in fact, had *not* been completed to the top. Now they faced two imperfect scenarios: they could either try to get all of their gear back to Dyea (in order to take the Chilkoot Trail), or they could start up the unfinished White Pass Trail and take their chances. One thing was sure: thousands of stampeders were just days behind them, and the longer they took, the more crowded, eroded, and dangerous both trails would become.

---

## LETTER FROM BOND'S FATHER IN CALIFORNIA TO PEARCE'S FATHER IN DENVER

Santa Clara, Cal.          Richard Pearce Esq.
Aug. 1. 1897.              Denver, Col.

My dear Sir,

I promised your son Stanley, when he sailed from Seattle, for Alaska, that I would write you concerning him and his departure for the Clondyke.

I arrived home yesterday and for the first time since he left I have leisure to write you.

I suppose he has written you of the phenomenal quantity of placer gold brought to Seattle.... I saw over a ton and a half of it weighed at the express office, and brought in in ore sacks....

Stanley and my son Marshall ... arrived in Seattle about the time the Portland came into port. Both of the boys soon became infected with the Clondyke fever, and I consented to let Marshall go there. Your son decided to join him as soon as he heard from you. As soon as my son in charge of my place here, read of the discoveries, he wired that he wished to go and would not take no for an answer. So I concluded to let him go also. The boys decided to buy their outfits together and to keep together. When they decided to go overland, which I thought the best way to go in ... I thought they would need some additional help and selected two men whom I outfitted on contract to go with them. ...

I bought most of their outfit, securing the best quality of the provisions taken, and getting the needed tools & hardware—

I also had three flat bottomed boats built in Seattle, then knocked down & tied up in bundles for packing. When they get over the Chilcoot Pass they will, in half a day, put their boats together, & be ready to go down the river—

Both of our sons are experienced in camping, packing & boating, as are two of the men I sent with them so I do not fear for their safety or ability to get through.

One of the men who has been over the route, & has been half his life a river boatman, has agreed with me to take all the boats through the rapids and let the young men walk around. I did this to please my wife rather than from any fear of any danger, for of all who have gone through not one has been injured.

Of clothes, each boy took two suits of Macinaw clothes, two Mackinaw shirts, some heavy woolen wrappers & drawers, & then each two pairs of light summer under clothes to wear under their heavy ones, as it saves washing the heavy ones which is difficult to do in winter.

Each had a double sleeping bag—pair of Alaska blankets, and fur robe 7 x 8 of lynx skin.

They had 18 months supply of provisions for the whole party, with plenty of evaporated potatoes, onions, and dried peaches, plums, apples, & apricots....

Stanley left in high spirits, & confident of his success—If one succeeds they all must as I believe they agreed to pool what they made, each taking one third.

I brought Stanley's trunk home with me at his request. He thought he might want it when he returned.

Mrs. Bond will see that his clothes are cared for, properly washed & kept from moths.

Yours truly

H. G. Bond

# DIFFERENT TIMES, DIFFERENT SPELLINGS

Throughout this book, multiple spellings are used for a number of places, such as the *Klondike* (*Klondyke* and *Clondyke*) and *Skagway* (*Skaguay*). The names of lakes might also be slightly different, such as *Lake Bennett* versus *Bennett Lake*. Even words such as *parka* (formerly *parkee*) have evolved since the 1890s. Another change is that Canada's Yukon Territory was officially carved out of the Northwest Territories in 1898.

# THE HORSE

# DEAD
# TRAIL

**N**o one can realize the hardships one has to undergo on a trip of this kind. The elements themselves seem to have a prejudice against us, and pouring rain has done all it can to make the trail almost impassable.

—STANLEY PEARCE

In Skagway, Stanley Pearce and Marshall Bond quickly struck a deal with two men named Cleveland and Young, owners of a small pack train of horses, to haul their supplies up the White Pass Trail for twelve and one-half cents per pound. Pearce put it this way: "We, by much diplomacy and considerable cash, managed to obtain the only horses . . . in the camp, and with 12 men as packers we started ahead regardless of the trail."

The six men at the core of the expedition were Pearce, Bond, Bailey, Wickman, Moore, and Louis Bond, who had just arrived on the S.S. *Mexico* with three horses and two dogs. In addition, Pearce and Bond hired six laborers from Juneau to help carry gear for $5 a day.

The expedition quickly developed a system for moving supplies up the trail as efficiently as possible. The horses each carried 150 pounds and were able to make the eighteen-mile ascent to the summit of White Pass in one day. Marshall Bond, who had experience with pack animals, accompanied the horses on trips to the summit and back down again.

The other men carried between 50 and 150 pounds on their backs in two- or three-mile segments. Pearce stayed below at base camp to guard supplies and cook for the packers. As supplies moved up the trail, the base camp gradually moved up as well. Their biggest challenge became the nonstop rain, which turned the trail into mud and slowed their progress.

"With the thousands who were coming," Bond wrote, "it was inevitable that the trail would soon be cut to pieces. . . . Our problem was to keep ahead of the crowd, and to do so we worked like dogs."

# Marshall Bond Diary

July 30, 1897.

Took out 9 horses of C & Y's. Trail bad and had several horses bogged down, but got through to the summit. Camped out for the night.

August 1, 1897.

Took nine of C & Y's horses and two of our own through to the summit. Arrived very tired. Had very little for supper. It was cold, so went to bed early. Fur robe slept in kept me warm.

Aug. 6, 1897.

Louis went with the pack train, as I had become foot sore. Went to Skaguay in the morning. Found a big crowd of men— recent arrivals . . . People staking out town lots.

"Lots of men have lost their nerve, sold out for a song, and started back for Seattle."

—Marshall Bond

The White Pass Trail often experienced traffic jams like this one.

## SKAGWAY, ALASKA, 6TH AUG. 1897

Dear Mother:

... We are all well & in good spirits, but had I known the tremendousness of the undertaking I would have searched for fortune in other fields. As it is I shall go thro' or break in two.... Our packing will cost us over $1000—and the balance of the money I shall hold to as well as possible. Father should count it lost for safety's sake & not build any castles on what we may make....

Don't worry, because we are in fine condition & equal to the hardships.

Affectionately,

Marshall

## SKAGAWAY, ALASKA. 6TH AUG. 1897.

Dear Mrs. Pearce:—

... The trail from here to the summit—about 18 miles—is sickening, and it is nothing to have half a dozen horses down at once. From the summit on its an open & easy country. A series of small lakes, connected, will enable us to make rapid progress with our things in a canoe, and then a six mile pack lands us at a lake which forms the head of the Yukon. While it looked very bleak for us for awhile I think now, we shall get our outfit thro by Sept. 1st, wh[ich] allows ample time for getting down the river before it freezes. We have undertaken a big task, but I now think

44

we can safely count ourselves through. Hundreds of men & horses arrive on every steamer, and the trail is lined with men staggering under every pound they can pack. Lots of men have lost their nerve, sold out for a song, and started back for Seattle. Our boats (taken apart) are daily moved forward with our camps. No one who hasn't experienced this trip can understand the obstacles to be overcome: its like an army campaign as one has to take clothing and a years provisions with one. While we have to work very hard there is no cause for worryment on your part as you might realize if you could see the amount of food we stow away at each meal. Mail is very uncertain, and while we will write you at every opportunity, you had better not write Stanley until we can give you some positive address....

With kind regards to Mr. Pearce, I am,

Sincerely Yours

Marshall Bond

## SKAGWAY BAY, AUG 9. 1897

Dearest Mother,

Many happy returns of the day. Bond tells me he wrote you the other day.

We are going through slowly but surely and working like fiends. I think nothing of making my 16 miles a day and am feeling fine. I have come down today to find a horse we had left behind and drive him up to camp, 12 miles from here.

This is an exciting life and I seem to be living a new life. Last night while looking up at the stars rolled snugly up in my sleeping bag I saw the grand Northern lights shooting up from a semicircle above the mountain and looking exactly like huge search lights shifting and cutting into space. It made me feel that now we were nearer the presence of our Maker than I had ever been before and I felt how small & trivial our small troubles & pleasures had been.

I am happy and ambitious, am confident of making a name for myself, and should I not find fortune it will make a man of me, and should I get through this trip I shall be able to undertake anything in the world.

Dearest love to you and all, dont worry about me if you dont hear.

I am the toughest looking customer you ever saw absolutely filthy & glad of it.

Your devoted son—

S. H. Pearce

> **"Should I not find fortune it will make a man of me, and should I get through this trip I shall be able to undertake anything in the world."**
>
> —Stanley Pearce

After Pearce and Bond reached the top of White Pass with all of their gear, the trail behind them went from bad to worse. An unfinished surface, constant rain, and heavy traffic created muddy and swampy areas. Horses got stuck in the mud, fell over, broke their legs, and were often left to die. Not long after Pearce and Bond reached the summit, the trail behind them was temporarily closed because of impassable conditions and rotting horseflesh.

# THE DENVER REPUBLICAN

The poor animals are the greatest sufferers. As a rule the men owning horses here have no knowledge of packing, of tying on packs, or managing horses. As an instance a short time ago I saw a man leading a horse. On one side of the saddle he had a large bundle, weighing about 100 pounds; on the other was a small box of about 25 pounds' weight, and in order to balance he had tied on in some way to the lighter side a granite boulder picked up along the road. But, aside from the ludicrous, it is a pitiful condition of affairs. And horses are strung all along the trail. A man only last evening borrowed an ax to put one poor animal out of misery, and two more were killed but 100 yards from our camp. . . .

—Stanley Pearce

Though it was an accomplishment in itself, reaching the summit of White Pass was no cause for great celebration. Over the next twenty-three days, the Pearce and Bond expedition still had to travel more than twenty miles by land and lake. By September 5, they had crossed into Canada and arrived at Lake Bennett, the headwaters of the Yukon River.

Pack horses were one of the great tragedies of the Klondike gold rush. Many of them did not survive. In their haste to find gold, many stampeders viewed the horses as expendable. In just a few months, an estimated three thousand horses died along this stretch of trail. Author Jack London later wrote, "The horses died like mosquitoes in the first frost, and from Skagway to Bennett they rotted in heaps." This is how the White Pass Trail also became known as the Dead Horse Trail.

# HEAD OF LAKE BENNET, N.W.T.
## SEPT. 5TH 1897.

Dearest Mother

We have finally reached this much looked for camping place after work and hardships I had little expected to encounter.

We have been just 33 days on the trail. It has rained for 28 days of the 33. I have walked over the trail three times each way averaging 8 miles a day and figuring up to about 250 miles. Half of that distance I have carried on my back not less than 50 pounds and at times as much as 100.

I have only told you this that I might also add that with all the hardships, exposure and hard work I feel in better health and spirits than ever, have gained in weight and am confident of being able to stand anything that this icy country can spring on me....

Our boats are all constructed and we are about to start down the lake....

We have two such fine dogs. We brought three rattling sleds and harness for the animals and hope to break them in shortly. They are called Pat & Jack and are devoted to Marshall and me.

We are rather proud of ourselves at having at last reached Lake Bennet. We are the first large outfit to come over this trail. There are 4000 people behind us and 1000 horses struggling over an almost impassable trail. Horses are dropping dead by tens and twenties and men are paying any sums for help to get to the lake.

We were also fortunate in packing our own boats over. They cost a good deal of money but we are fully repaid as we have the best built boats on the lake.

During the height of the gold rush, tens of thousands of men hauled gear up the steep Chilkoot Pass, which included this dreaded ascent up the 1,500 "Golden Stairs" that were carved into the winter ice. After dropping off their heavy loads at the top of the Golden Stairs, miners slid down to the bottom to get another load.

> **"I feel in better health and spirits than ever, have gained in weight and am confident of being able to stand anything that this icy country can spring on me."**
>
> —Stanley Pearce

I do hope we shall find something to repay us for our hard work.... Our only fear is now of winter setting in earlier than usual and the consequent freezing over of the Yukon....

We shall probably have lots of spare time on our hands during some of the winter months. We have a small library. Marshall and I purchased before leaving, a bible, Plutarch's lives, Shakespeare, Socrates Apology, Homer's Iliad and, for light reading Kiplings late poems which I am immensely fond of. We shall probably know them all by heart before reaching civilization....

One immense satisfaction to me, in fact to Marshall as well is that we are on British soil and under British rule. A detachment of mounted police is here at the lake. Fine looking fellows, one feels perfectly safe that one's property and life is safe....

Would you believe that it were possible to live on Beans,

bacon & bread (3 B's) three times a day for 33 days without change? I have done [so] and thrive and am getting hungry for more beans now.

We have had about 12 men packing for us and had to feed them therefore we were unable to produce any of our luxuries for fear of losing them all.

The scenery here is indescribably grand. Surrounded by rugged snow capped peaks, huge glaciers here and there[,] the head waters of the Yukon is really an imposing sight. The snow has been gradually creeping down on us and the nights are beginning to get quite cold.

Marshall & I have hardened ourselves by plunging into all the small lakes we have camped beside and I am now prepared to tackle an iceberg with impunity....

I think of you both so much and with such fond and loving wishes.

May God bless you both and keep you well and strong. Goodbye.

Your devoted son,

Stanley H. Pearce

Stanley Pearce and Marshall Bond were fortunate to be on the front lines of the Klondike gold rush. The vast majority of stampeders arrived at Lake Bennett after it was already frozen. That winter, an estimated thirty thousand people were forced to camp out near the frozen lakes. They formed temporary tent cities, built thousands of boats, and waited for the spring day when the frozen Yukon River would finally melt back into water.

# DOWN
# YUK

# THE
# ON

**W**ords could not describe it. . . . The scenery was by far the grandest I have ever seen. . . . Bond & I spied a bear while floating down the river and tried to land but failed. Wild swans, geese & ducks were everywhere. Indian camps by scores . . .

—STANLEY PEARCE

Lake Bennett, headwaters of the mighty Yukon River

Shortly after the expedition arrived at Lake Bennett, the six laborers from Juneau received their pay and headed back down the trail toward Skagway. On September 7, the remaining six embarked on the next leg of their journey: a five-hundred-mile trip, in thirty-foot wooden boats, across a series of lakes and down the Yukon River.

Pearce and Bond shared one boat, Louis and Moore another, and Bailey and Wickman the third. Their goal was to reach Dawson City before the Yukon River froze, which usually occurred sometime in mid-October. Everyone on the expedition knew they would be cutting it close.

## Marshall Bond Diary

September 7, 1897

Sails & boats completed about noon. After luncheon loaded the boats. At 3 p.m. we pulled out. . . . A breeze from the south carried us down the lake and at last we were off. About 9 p.m. it was quite dark. . . . We came to a tiny bay just large enough to hold us. So rocky we slept on flour bags. After a supper turned in.

September 8, 1897

Pulled out at 7 a.m. Sailed about 4 miles. When wind breezes so strong & waves so high we deemed it unsafe to continue further in boats so overloaded.

September 9, 1897

Wind was too strong. . . . Several boats passed & went on

down the lake, but it is only too evident that while our boats may be adapted for river work, they sit too low in the water to ride a rough lake.

SEPTEMBER 11, 1897

Bailey & I whip-sawed most all day, and by 3 p.m. had all the boards needed to raise each boat a board higher.

At Lake Bennett, most stampeders had to cut down trees, whipsaw them into boards (above), and try to build sturdy boats. Because many of these men had no previous experience building boats, a number of their boats leaked, and some even sank.

Sept. 15th 97.

Under the Union Jack at
mounted Police Station, foot of Taguh
lake.

Dearest Mother    We have reached
here safe & very well. Our boats
have acted well in very stormy weather
and the worst of our sailing exp. is
over. We pd. duty and are ready to
start further. We bought fresh
mutton here & look for a feast.
I am splendidly well & in great
spirits. One snow storm has
struck us & nights are cold. I
have developed into a famous
skipper & sail a boat like a
veteran. I send this by Richardson
who goes into report favorably on
telegraph station here. Write me,
"Stewart River, North West Terr.
Government establishes Station there.
Dearest love. The worst is over
& now we must make a fortune
after so many trials. I am enjoying
a grand experience. Grand Scenery
Perfect health & am certain of success

Tell Father that

Your devoted Son
Stanley Pearce

## September 15th 97.
## Under the Union Jack at Mounted Police
## Station foot of Tagish lake

Dearest Mother

We have reached here safe & very well. Our boats have acted well in very stormy weather and the worst of our sailing exp. is over. We p[ai]d. duty and are ready to start further. We bought fresh mutton here & look for a feast. I am splendidly well & in great spirits. One snow storm has struck us & nights are cold. I have developed into a famous skipper & sail a boat like a veteran....

Dearest love. The worst is over & now we must make a fortune after so many trials.

Tell father that I am enjoying a grand experience. Grand scenery Perfect health & am certain of success.

Your devoted son

Stanley Pearce

# THE DENVER REPUBLICAN

The Canadian government will construct a telegraph line passing through here on the way to Dawson City and other points in the Klondyke region. . . . There are 11 Canadian policemen here, and 20 more are expected to-morrow. Posts will be established and maintained every 50 miles and mail carried from point to point. In this way it is proposed to keep in operation a mail line from Yukon river points to tidewater during the whole of the winter. . . .

—Stanley Pearce

# LETTER FROM STANLEY PEARCE
## DESCRIBING EVENTS ON SEPT. 16.

Dawson City—N.W.T.

Dear Father & Mother,

   . . . To begin with I sent you a scribbled few lines from Tagish Lake where the Customs officials held us up reducing our cash supply considerably.

   I believe I said to you then, that our travelling from there on would be easy and free from danger or trouble. If I could but have seen ahead!! Only three hours after that our three boats, each manned by two men, Marshall Bond and I running one, myself at the helm, hoisted our sails and with a stiff wind behind sailed out into Lake Marsh.

   We had no sooner got well out into the middle of the lake which is 10 miles wide and 35 miles long, when the wind began to whistle and howl and my strength was taxed to the utmost holding the boat with head before the wind, the waves soon were running tremendously high and should we have swung into the trough swamping the boats was inevitable. The wind increased and I soon became exhausted. Bond in someway took my place and braced himself for the hardest effort he ever had. One of our boats ahead of us was manned by Bailey & Wickman. We saw to our dismay their mast and sail go with a crash and as we passed flying we almost gave them up for lost. Bailey jumped to the oars and both shook off their boots. Our other boat had hugged the left shore and were out of the worst of the storm. Soon, I, while holding the sail rope ready to loosen should our sail go, I heard

Bond grunt and groan with his efforts. You see our steering gear consisted of nothing but a large oar and required a tremendous effort for us to hold the boat. Soon he shouted "Stanley I am afraid its all up". The waves were splashing over our stern and things looked pretty rocky.

Finally Marshall said "Sing Stanley and I may hold her". So off I started "El Capitan" march, all the Yale songs I could think of, Marshall joining in lustily. Every second we expected to go; but with the singing and good cheer Marshall kept up his strength and as we had pointed at a cove in an arm some 10 miles ahead we finally made a landing. Bond & I shook hands and said we would not go through that again for all the gold in the Klondike. I, at once got out our field glasses and saw our boat which had lost sail on the right shore rowing for dear life to keep before the wind. The third boat joined us. The following day we made the foot of the lake where we had to wait 36 hours for our men on the right shore, who had crossed over and not finding us and finding a pair of oars on the shore had given us up for lost. We then resumed our journey....

> **"Bond & I shook hands and said we would not go through that again for all the gold in the Klondike."**
>
> —Stanley Pearce

The Whitehorse Rapids was one of the most dangerous sections of the trip. During the gold rush, large rocks and rapidly flowing water destroyed more than one hundred boats and claimed a number of lives.

ARSS & D
PHOTOS
DAWSON.

2164.

After their close call on Lake Marsh, the six men continued down the Yukon River. When they reached a red warning flag, they pulled the three boats ashore and walked downriver to inspect the rapids at Miles Canyon.

"The river narrows to about 50 feet," Pearce wrote, "and rushes through between walls of basalt of perfect column structure which are from 50 to 150 feet high. The velocity of the water is so great that the center of the stream is about 15 feet higher than the sides. We decided to hire three men to take our boats through and I took the first boat as a passenger. What a grand ride! I timed the trip and we went through a measured ¾ of a mile in one minute & 7 seconds.

"The other boats came through safely.

"The Rapids two miles below," Pearce continued, "were even more exciting and far more dangerous."

When the expedition reached the treacherous Whitehorse Rapids, the stampeders unloaded their supplies and hired some men to steer their boats through the fast-moving water. Everyone decided to walk around the rapids except for Pearce, who chose to ride again in one of the boats for fun.

"None of the rest of our party cared to undertake the ride," Pearce wrote. "It was simply grand our boats were tossed around like matches in the great combs of the rapids; but outside of a thorough wetting and a narrow squeak as we grazed a rock . . . we had no mishap. However the men who saw our boats through said as I shook hands and said goodbye that that would be their last trip."

Marshall Bond, meanwhile, paid a family of Indians to help carry their supplies down to the end of the rapids. "I hired the services of four Indians who were camped there," Bond wrote.

During the gold rush, many local Indians were hired to carry supplies.

"The Indians were an old man, ill with tuberculosis, two boys of about twelve and fourteen respectively, and a little girl who could not have been over eight or ten.

"It was a sloppy cold day with an occasional flurry of snow. The Indians were thinly clad, and wore moose hide moccasins without socks. The old man toook [took] fifty pounds at a load; the two boys one hundred each; and the little girl fifty. . . . When she had her load fastened to her back I had to lift both her and her load for her to get on her feet. Once on her feet she packed with apparent ease and kept up with the rest of us. At the end of the trip our men had a fire and some hot tea for us."

Further downriver, the expedition encountered more people. "We camped near a band of Indians from whom we bought some moccasins and fish," Bond recalled. "They had brush lean-tos or pieces of canvas slanted back from a frame to the ground under which they took shelter, and in front of which they kept a fire going in order to keep warm as they had scarcely any bedding. They alternated between short periods of sleep and getting up and adding to the fire."

## LETTER FROM STANLEY PEARCE TO PARENTS

... We reached the foot of LaBarge and were soon fairly launched on the swift running Yukon. Nothing very exciting happened for some time, our only difficulty being the very hard landings in swift water and almost impossibility of keeping the boats together.

The weather by this time had become very much colder and

the sloughs and small streams running into the Yukon were frozen over.

White river when we passed it was throwing huge ice floes into the Yukon and made our journey much more difficult, and when we reached Stewart River we found that throwing even more ice.... From there down the river which had widened to almost a mile was choked with running ice, swift running and dangerous. While we floated with it the danger was not so great but landing was a tremendous effort. And we almost gave up going any further until ice was solid and we could sled down.

# MARSHALL BOND DIARY

SEPTEMBER 28, 1897

Cloudy & a little snow. Thermom. 23°... Got a late start—8:30. Arrived Fort Selkirk (mouth Pelly River) 9:30. Some Indians live there & a small store is running.

SEPTEMBER 30, 1897

On down the river. Stopped for luncheon just below White River. It was pouring a vast amount of ice. When we passed Stewart River found it pouring ice too. Camped about 10 miles below it.

OCTOBER 1, 1897

Flowing ice made travel difficult & dangerous.... Some men on their way out—told us of a great scarcity of grub in Dawson.

After dropping down from the coastal mountains, the Yukon River flows through flatter, open country toward Dawson City.

OCTOBER 2, 1897

Boats frozen in, & we had to cut out to mid-stream. Got started about 11:30 . . . A number of people on this way out as they had no grub.

OCTOBER 3, 1897

Took boats out of water & put them on top of ice. Piled cargoes ashore. Spent day reading & chatting. Cooked dinner myself. Had roast beef hash, boiled potatoes, & apple dumplings. So cold bread freezes, & oatmeal when fried cooks on outside and remains frozen inside.

OCTOBER 4, 1897

Bailey & I explored the island we were on, & crossed to the mainland. After luncheon we went hunting. Saw some bear signs but got nothing larger than a grouse.

OCTOBER 5, 1897

Ran 10 miles or more in lots of ice & landed for night with difficulty.

OCTOBER 6, 1897

We discovered two men building a cabin on our island. They said we were only 15 miles from Dawson. . . . Many boats passed.

OCTOBER 7, 1897

Rose early & pulled out. Had great difficulty for about ½ a mile w[ith]. keeping off the shore, owing to the current. . . . On way met several men walking along shore with packs on their

backs. They were on the way to Henderson Creek. Arrived . . .
about 3:30 p.m . . .

In evening walked over to Dawson. . . . Took in Dance Halls
& Gambling rooms. Plenty of gold.

Pearce and Bond's outfit of six men, two dogs, and thousands of pounds of supplies had finally reached Dawson City. After leaving Lake Bennett, they had braved high winds and waves on the lakes, navigated treacherous rapids on the river, and managed to avoid large, dangerous chunks of ice. With the Yukon River about to freeze completely, they had arrived just in time.

Now, eighty-two days after seeing the miners arrive in Seattle, Pearce and Bond were camped on the outskirts of Dawson City. After dinner that night, they wandered into the legendary frontier town and stepped into the Dominion Saloon for a drink.

For nearly three months, Pearce had enjoyed needling Bond about how ragged and unkempt he looked. But when Pearce sat down at the bar that night and finally saw his own reflection in a mirror, he didn't know what to say. He was staring at a dirty, disheveled man with a big red beard, darkened skin, a dirty shirt, and a tattered coat. "My God!" Pearce exclaimed. "Is that me?"

"It is," Bond replied, "and how much handsomer do you regard yourself than the individual beside you?"

Pearce apologized to his friend, invited him to a drink, and criticized him no more.

# WELCOME
# DAWS

#32. The River Front. Dawson City.

Dawson City sits on a flat piece of land where the Yukon and Klondike Rivers meet. In 1897 most of the restaurants, saloons, dance halls, and stores were located on the two blocks along the riverfront.

# TO
# ON CITY

**T**here is the usual
row of saloons
and dance halls
thronged with men. Gold
dust alone is used and
sacks are thrown over the
bar and into the gamblers'
hands unceasingly. Men
are all dressed in
mackinaws, fur caps—
long Kackee coats lined
with fur, [and] moccasins.

—STANLEY PEARCE

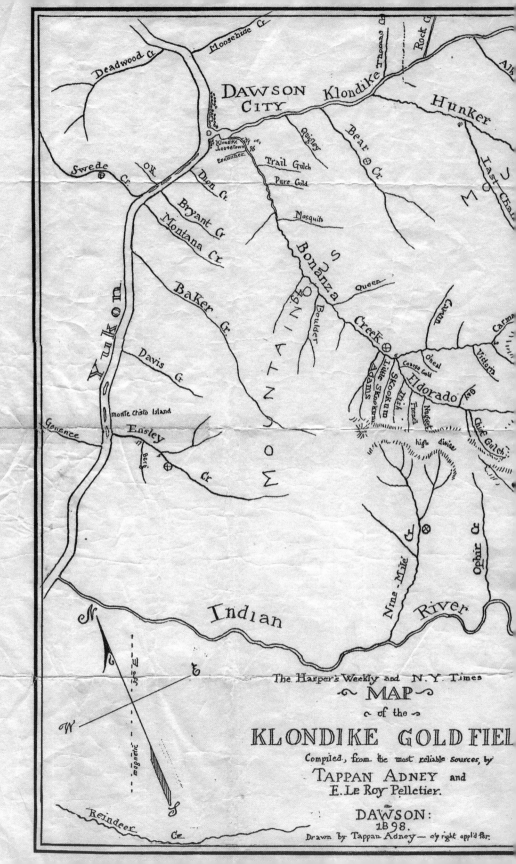

The Harper's Weekly and N.Y. Times
~ MAP ~
~ of the ~
KLONDIKE GOLD FIEL
Compiled, from the most reliable sources, by
TAPPAN ADNEY and
E. Le Roy Pelletier.
DAWSON:
1898.
Drawn by Tappan Adney — c'y right appl'd for.

Marshall Bond (far left) and Stanley Pearce (far right) sit in front of their cabin.
This is only one of two known photos from Pearce and Bond's entire expedition.

In one of his letters, Stanley Pearce made this sketch to show the location of
their cabin.

*U*pon arrival in Dawson City, Pearce and Bond's expedition divided into two groups. Bailey, Wickman, and Moore traveled up Bonanza Creek, built a cabin at the mouth of Skookum Gulch, and started looking for gold. Throughout the winter, the two groups would keep in touch and visit each other on a regular basis.

As planned, Stanley Pearce and the two Bond brothers stuck together. On their first day in Dawson, they met a journalist from New York named John McGillivray. The following day they bought a small log cabin with him for $750. The thirteen-by-sixteen-foot cabin had one main room, a front porch, and double windows, which were a luxury in the Klondike. The cabin was located near the river, next to a hospital, and just a short walk from downtown.

After living out of a tent for more than two months, Pearce and the Bond brothers lost no time settling into their new home. They dismantled their boats and used the boards to build bunk beds. They also built a cache, or storage room, onto the outside of the cabin to store extra food and supplies. Inside the cabin was a kerosene lamp, which would provide light at night and during the long, dark winter days.

DAWSON CITY, NWT. OCTOBER 11TH, 1897.

Dear Mother: —

We arrived several days ago well etc. Have bought a cabin with a New York Herald Correspondent and as our party will not always be together, it will be large enough. We are moving in and hope to be comfortably settled in a day or two. Great scarcity of food prevails and we keep ours under lock and key all the time....

The mines have not started working yet, so it is not as lively as ordinarily. Still gold is everywhere; gold dust is the currency of the country and every one carries a sack. The tributaries of the Klondike are pretty well located. Many people are discouraged. Louis, Stanley and I are not....

Good order obtains here and last night twenty additional mounted police arrived. There are a number of nice women in town and quite a number of fine fellows. I doubt if the mail service contemplated will get in operation this winter. However, I shall have opportunity of sending out letters occasionally over the ice by men going out up the river....

We have had a long arduous trip and one not devoid of peril. I am glad it is over at last. We are now as snug as a bug in a rug. Send any mail which may come for us to Dawson, Goodbye,

Affectionately Yours,

Marshall.

Pearce and Bond made it a point to meet well-connected people in Dawson. Hoping to gain inside information that might lead them to gold, they befriended miners, businessmen, and government officials. They dined in restaurants, frequented saloons, and invited guests to their cabin for meals and card games.

During their first week in Dawson, Pearce and Bond met a young businessman named L.W. Fox. Fox had a considerable amount of money, claims on various creeks, and plans to create a large mining company. Fox met regularly with Pearce and Bond to keep them posted on opportunities he might have for them.

# STAKING
# A CLAIM

"When prospectors found a promising spot, they staked a claim by placing posts at each corner, one with their name and date on it. The prospector then had three days to go to town and file a legal claim. Because the claims were usually measured by crude means, disagreements over exact boundaries were common.

"The first claim in a new location was called the 'discovery claim.' Subsequent claims were legally referred to by their relationship to this claim, along with the name of the creek— 5 Above Eldorado, or 6 Below Bonanza, for example."

—Museum at the Klondike Gold Rush National
Historical Park–Seattle

The Canadian North-West Mounted Police were legendary for being tough and keeping order in frontier towns.

# Marshall Bond Diary

October 12, 1897

In evening met with L. W. Fox . . . He seemed like a bright agreeable young chap.

October 13, 1897

Met Fox in a.m. & brought him to our cabin . . . Fox offered us a "lay" on #5 below Discovery on Bonanza. He also thought he could give us work on El Dorado.

## Oct. 18th 1897. Dawson City—N.W.T.

Dear Father & Mother,

. . . I have not yet been up the Klondike to the diggings and cant fairly form any opinion. I have however talked a great deal with the few mining men who are here and found out so much. . . .

There is no doubt plenty of gold here and some of the claims fabulously rich. I have seen already more gold dust than ever before; but the average yield of the claims will be small. . . .

I am confident myself of making money. . . . Marshall started off this morning to be gone a few days with . . . Fox, one of the principal holders of rich diggings. Louis Bond & I are watching the Cabin. Louis starts off tomorrow, leaving me alone. I am already a fair cook but my bread ... well, I have to plead with the dogs to eat it with me.

The feeling of living in a cabin of my own is a pleasant sensation. I have had several rattling games of piquet with a young Britisher named Van Milligin....

I can truly say to both of you dear parents, that I am happy, contented, & confident ... as I am fond of this adventurous life....

With fond love your devoted son

Stanley H. Pearce

# Meeting Jack London

One day in mid-October, two men pitched a tent near Pearce and Bond's cabin. One of them was a twenty-one-year-old adventurer from California named Jack London. After the gold rush, London would become one of the most famous authors of the twentieth century, thanks in part to writing stories set in the Klondike.

Jack London camped near Pearce and Bond's cabin until early December. For a month and a half, he stored his food in their cache and spent time in their cabin, warming up, talking politics, and sipping hot drinks. London enjoyed both of their dogs but was particularly intrigued by the one named Jack, a Saint Bernard mix with a strong work ethic. Jack would later become the inspiration for Buck, the canine protagonist in London's famous novel *The Call of the Wild*.

Jack London is the young, clean-shaven man between the tree stumps (wearing cap, hand in pocket). London traveled over the Chilkoot Trail and arrived in Dawson City a few weeks after Pearce and Bond.

> "We are now as snug as a bug in a rug."
>
> —Marshall Bond

## Marshall Bond Diary

OCTOBER 24, 1897

Fox & I got two dogs & a sledge & drove them up Bonanza.... On return went down to Skookum Gulch & saw Bailey, Wick, & Moore. Bailey sinking a hole, & the other two building a cabin.

NOVEMBER 3, 1897

Pearce & McGillivray started up Bonanza on a trip to take in the mining country. Fox working on some mining deals. He ... is not afraid to take chances.

## DAWSON CITY, NOV. 5TH, 1897.

Dear Father:—

... Gold is found almost everywhere, though not always in paying quantities, but it shows the country is mineralized and it is not reasonable to think that Eldorado and Bonanza Creeks will be the only paying ones. But prospecting is slow and arduaous [arduous], and it will twke [take] time to demonstrate the values of other creeks. Eldorado is the richest creek....

The most prominent figure is Alexander McDonald, a laborer of Scotch extraction. He bought a claim on Eldorado last year for $300.00 and made a lot of money.... In one day he took $30,000 out of the ground....

Love to all,

Affectionately Yours,

Marshall.

## MARSHALL BOND DIARY

NOVEMBER 5, 1897

Bailey started for Skookum after breakfast. Fox detained by business. Has bought remaining half of #5 below on Bonanza for $15000. Expects to go out on first ice & wants me to represent him in his absence.

NOVEMBER 7, 1897

Agreed to take charge of Fox's property & represent him while he is out, for $15.00 per day. I have the disposal of my own time. While I ordinarily would use it for him, I am to act for myself if needs be.

NOVEMBER 17, 1897

Long talk with Jack London on Socialism. Fox starts out over the ice tomorrow. Wrote some letters and straightened out Fox's papers in my charge. Plain talk with McG.

22° below zero. Walked down town in morning. On the way a fellow told me my nose was frozen. Rubbed snow on it, & with my bare hand. On my way back met Louis, stopped to tell him of my mishap, and discovered his nose frozen.

November 19, 1897

Some of the El Dorado mining men were in town and were celebrating. . . . About $3,000- worth of champagne drunk.

With L.W. Fox on his way to the United States and England in search of investors, Marshall Bond was now in charge of claim No. 17 Eldorado, which was located up Eldorado Creek, about seventeen miles outside of Dawson City. Bond would spend much of the winter there in a small mining cabin, although he would still make frequent trips back and forth to Dawson by dogsled.

> "Walked down town in morning. On the way a fellow told me my nose was frozen."
>
> —Marshall Bond

# Marshall Bond Diary

November 25, 1897

20 to 30 below zero . . . Thanksgiving dinner, beans, potatoes, bread. . . . Bailey & Moore dropped in. Played cards.

November 26, 1897

39° below 0 . . . Pulled out 10:15 arrived town 2 p.m. Tho' a cold day was quite comfortable travelling. Found "Opera House" "The Dominion" & the "Dance Hall" burned down.

Copy of mining agreement between Marshall Bond and L.W. Fox. Jack London and Louis Bond signed as witnesses.

# DEC. 1ST, 1897—
## DAWSON CITY—N.W.T.

Dearest Mother

... To give you an idea of how much we mind the cold here I will describe a trip Marshall and I have just made. Last week we were confidentially informed of a rich strike on a new creek some 25 miles up the Klondike. We made up our minds to investigate and stake our claim if we thought it advisable. Early Sunday morning in pitch darkness we crawled out of our fur robes and after starting the fire I took a look at the thermometer outside and announced to Marshall that it was only 40° below zero, which meant 50° below on the river. We put up three days rations of bacon, hard tack and tea, a sack of horse meat for the dogs, and this with our rifles (we hoped to run across a moose or caribou) and fur robes made up the sled load. I was dressed as follows— a suit of Jaeger flannels, heavy mackinaw shirt, and suit of mackinaw trousers and coat. Two pair of socks, small arctic socks, and heavy german socks, over which I wore moose skin moccasins. Moose skin mittens with fur border covered my hands, and a marten skin cap coming down over the ears and back of the neck. Over all this I wore what is called a parkee, made of drilling. It is exactly like a huge night shirt with a hood to it, the hood being edged with fox tails. This parkee comes a little below the knees and is very light and splendidly warm. In order to protect the nose and cheeks I tied a handkerchief across my nose, so that finally nothing but my eyes were exposed to the cold wind.

This is absolutely necessary; as I found afterwards, as one day my handkerchief being frozen solid it dropped down and I went the rest of the day without it. My nose was frozen several times as also were my cheeks. Brisk rubbing with snow would soon warm the frozen parts however and the only harm done was that my nose and cheeks both felt as if they had been badly burnt.

We soon had breakfast and, having hitched up the two dogs started at break of day. The dogs were cold and went fast and we made the 12 miles to our first stopping place, the mouth of Hunker creek in two hours and a half, almost record time....

The place where we stopped is a half way house for points on the creek and the first night we stopped there, there were a dozen others with six or eight dogs—all scrambling to cook over the small stove. We rolled up in our furs on the ground and had a wretched night. We were off again before daylight it being still colder, the thermometer reading in town 60 below that morning. The dogs were anxious to go fast and we tore up the Klondike. It was most exhilarating. The sun does not show itself now, but when we reached the creek we were bound for we could see the "rockies" in the distance tinted with the most beautiful colors. Everything was solitude,—not an animal, not a sound and Bond and I both paused from the hard work we had in hand to comment on the grandeur of it all and wonder what unknown thing made this Godforsaken barren country so fascinating to us. Perhaps it was the feeling akin to that which explorers in unknown countries have; but the fact remains with all its hardships there is a certain indescribable ghastly fascination about it all. We were obliged to break away from our meditations and make our way up the lonely creek. It was awfully hard work ploughing through the snow but we finally arrived at the discovery stake on the creek.

We found several locations had been made; the creek however looked so small and unpromising that we decided not to throw away our right to stake anywhere on whole the Klondike district by locating at this point so[,] disappointed[,] we started back and reaching the Klondike just as it was growing dusk hitched up our shivering dogs and made back to Hunker, having travelled about twenty five miles since our breakfast of bacon & hard tack. We spent another night at the "hog ranch" as Marshall and I called the place. Twenty men slept in the cabin that night. Marshall & I . . . talked ourselves to sleep with reminiscences of good dinners & civilized comforts, and dozed off with dogs at our feet, heads and on top of us. We were the first up in the morning—and with a shout to the dogs, went tearing down the Klondike with the stars glittering in the heavens. With a snatch of a song now and then bursting from one or the other of us—an occasional shout as our moccasined feet slipped from under us on the slippery ice we made rattling good time, anxious to reach our comfortable cabin and fill ourselves with a comfortable clean mess of food. We made the 12 miles in 2 hours . . . and if any one of you think that is not fast let him try it in Denver. We were none the worse for the trip. My muscles ached a little from the long fast travelling, but a good night's rest made me feel in splendid condition and ready for another trip. I never was in better health or condition, without boasting, am as strong as a bull. Of course we both get fits of the blues; but generally we are happy and contented. I find the greatest comfort in living in the future; picturing myself in the luxuries and comforts of home with you all whom I hold so dear. . . . I was fifteen miles up Bonanza creek the other day on my way to visit one of the Bonanza kings. I stopped in at a cabin to warm myself and rest for half an hour, where I found out that it was my birthday. My thoughts immediately took wing—and I pictured you all at dinner....

Dawson is a sad looking place now. First a fire burnt out the little church destroying several men's outfits.... A second fire started on the eve of Thanksgiving about midnight. It was bitterly cold—40 below—a masked ball was in full swing at the Opera House. I was awakened by Louis Bond who shouted there was a big fire in town. I hurriedly dressed threw on my parkee and ran down. It was a grand though terrible sight; five houses burnt— together with the opera house. The houses were the principal saloons....

One of the mounted police and I rescued four little puppies from under a burning floor, and turned them over to a kind hearted woman. For a time it seemed that everything would go including the stores. But willing hands tore down small shacks on either side of the big blaze and there being no wind the fire burnt itself out. I returned to the cabin about five in the morning where I found a roaring fire in the stove—hot coffee ready—and several of us sat around and discussed the situation, drifted off to hard luck stories generally and finally turned in for a snooze about eight....

I must finish this up as I may be very busy the next few days hauling wood, running up the creek etc. and I am anxious for this letter to get out at once.

Dearest love to all—I am taking splendid care of myself and there is no cause for worry.

I will send word again at the first opportunity.

Your devoted son

Stanley H. Pearce.

# Dawson City, N.W.T.
## Dec. 9th 1897

Dear Father and Mother

This letter goes out over the trail tomorrow or the next day. The weather has moderated here considerably of late and the thermometer has hung about the zero mark for some days.

Marshall and I took advantage of the warm spell and cut and hauled a good quantity of firewood. It is very hard work as we are forced to go across the Yukon, well up into the hills, and bring the heavy logs down through some two feet of snow....

The sun showed itself at ten minutes to one the other day—and set again at ten minutes past one.

At ten o'clock one can just see and at half past three it is quite dark. After the 21st however the days begin to lengthen rapidly and we will soon have an end of this expensive coal oil existence....

The Govt. Mail is expected in every day. How glad I shall be if I get good tidings between now and Xmas. Not a word have I heard since leaving Seattle. The longest time I have ever been without hearing from home....

I would write to others were we not so hard up for paper and ink. We are forced to limit our correspondence to home letters, as one cannot buy paper here at any price....

With very much love to all of you and best wishes for Xmas ...
Goodbye—
Your devoted son

Stanley H. Pearce.

DAWSON Y.T

During the long Klondike winter, dogsleds were the primary form of transportation.

Dear Father

In explanation for drawing on you [withdrawing money from a bank account] for $552.00 through the Alaska Commercial Company I write you briefly.... When drawing I remembered your repeated request never to draw; but it was the only way in which I could raise the very necessary amount. When Bond returns from Eldorado I will get from him the detailed account of our expenses to date which were far heavier than ... either of us anticipated. After our arrival here we had to meet heavy expenses in getting our cabin for the winter, buying up extra supplies which we were short of, getting necessary furs & moccasins—all at fabulous prices. All these things I will put together as an expense account. From now on our expenses will be nil— Our income at present is $660.00 per month which however has to be rocked out [separated] from the pay dirt on an Eldorado claim #17—which Bond and I are looking after for the owner Fox—who has gone out.... Marshall and I are on the alert for anything that may turn up. We are hopeful and yet not too confident. I am writing you and Mother another letter in which I speak more generally of what we are doing etc. I beg you will honor my draft Father and I shall work and scheme to try if not to make a fortune at least to pull out even and return to you your handsome advance.

Your very affectionate son

Stanley H. Pearce

# DAWSON, N.W.T.
## DEC. 16TH 97.

Dearest Mother

... Tomorrow morning ... Lewis [Louis] Bond goes up the
Yukon 70 miles to Henderson creek [,] a new discovery, where we
have acquired interests in eleven claims. Marshall is at present
at Eldorado creek, 20 miles away, and I shall be left alone at the
cabin. I must say things look promising for us here. We have been
keeping very quiet about are [our] affairs and now stand in very
close with the one or two leading men of the district....

I very rarely while at home go to Dawson proper. It is such a
deadly place. Nothing but gin mills & gambling dens. Now and
then one of us takes a turn about town to pick up the latest news.

In regard to stampedes and new discoveries we are well
posted.... Of course all these things may amount to nothing,
should that be the case I will accept the inevitable with good grace.
However it seems to me that with six or eight months before us;
during which time we will have been everywhere, seen everything
and can be called old timers, that when the great rush of people
arrive here in the spring we should be able to realize something.
Our great drawback is the lack of ready cash. Instead of arriving
here with three or four thousand dollars as we expected to do—we
were almost out of cash when we got here. Then we had to buy a
cabin, get more grub, lay in firewood etc. etc. at exorbitant prices.
... I do hope we will be successful, as one surely deserves a great
deal of recompense for what we have gone through....

Your devoted son

Stanley H. Pearce.

## "Stanley & I each got an icicle in our stocking"

—Marshall Bond

---

### DAWSON CITY
### 17TH DEC. 1897.

Dear Mother:—

...A week from tonight is Christmas Eve. I hope Fox will get the little nuggets to you in time. They dont amount to anything, but were the best I could pick up at so short a notice....

Love to all, A Merry Christmas & Happy New Year.

Affectionately yours,

Marshall

---

### DAWSON CITY
### 30TH DEC. 1897.

Dear Mother:—

...Christmas was a most enjoyable day.... Stanley & I each got an icicle in our stocking—kind remembrances from one another....

We have struck pay dirt on Fox's El Dorado lay. I panned two pans wh[ich] went $25. and $15. respectively. I could see the coarse gold in the dirt.... I hope we shall make some money here, and am inclined to think we shall....

Affectionately yours,

Marshall

# MARSHALL BOND DIARY

Jan 1/98. . . . Started the phonograph immediately upon rising & we had music all day. . . . Attended masquerade ball.

---

## JANUARY 5TH, 1898

Dear Mother:

... Quite a bit of scurvy* in camp. The doctor says it is due largely to wretchedly cooked food & a lack of personal cleanliness. You know that neither of these is possible with me, so no fear. I take my morning cold bath regularly. . . .

Stanley & I with a sled & the dogs have been working all day cutting & hauling wood, & I am good & tired in consequence, but we have enough to last two weeks. Stanley, Capt. Harper, & I dined at Bowie's tonight. Soup, roast beef, peas, maccoroni [macaroni], chutney bread & butter, mince pie—WOW!! They are playing hearts, but I excused myself to finish this, as I have to go back to El Dorado tomorrow morning.

Have bought out the interest of McGillivray in our cabin. We did not hit it off any too well. . . .

The sun ... gets up above the horizon high enough to give us a wink between twelve and one. . . . Must turn in. With love & best wishes for the New Year. I am

Affectionately Yours,

Marshall.

---

*Scurvy is a disease caused by a lack of vitamin C in one's diet. Symptoms include extreme weakness, swollen and bleeding gums, and bleeding under the skin.

# Dawson, Jan 6th 1898

Dear Father

...Am splendidly well. Xmas day was rather dull; but Marshall and I had a great spread at Bowie's, our neighbor. "Absent friends" caused a glisten in nearly every eye. New Year's Eve was also passed at Bowie's with grand festivities. He is awfully good to me and has been the means of driving away many a lonesome hour....

I am now in the delightful position of being flat busted—and I rather like the sensation. Bond is very near it being only able to hit the $90.00 mark....

Best love to all. We are all well. No mail or news from the outside has arrived yet. I hope my letters arrived O.K.— Don't send any newspapers they won't get here. Clippings of interest would be very welcome.

Goodbye— Trust you all are in the best of health.

Happy New Year!

Your affectionate son

Stanley H. Pearce

Ironically, one of Pearce and Bond's biggest obstacles to finding gold turned out to be money. Even though they had left Seattle with more than $5,000 in cash and a well-equipped outfit, Pearce and Bond had spent a significant amount transporting everything, paying customs duties, and buying the cabin. Compared with successful gold miners and businessmen like L.W. Fox, Pearce and Bond were relatively poor.

Another obstacle to finding gold was the fact that most of the valuable pieces of land had already been staked. Pearce and Bond arrived in Dawson more than a year after the initial discovery in 1896. This meant that the men who had already been working and living in the Yukon Valley had staked out the best claims long ago.

Despite these challenges, Pearce and the Bond brothers remained optimistic that their connections, hard work, and savvy would eventually pay off.

"With all its hardships there is a certain indescribable ghastly fascination about it all."

—Stanley Pearce

# THE SEA FOR

Placer gold is gold that is mixed in the ground with gravel, sand, and sediment. Using rocker boxes (shown above) was one way that miners separated out gold.

# RCH
# GOLD

Quite a number regretted going to Swede creek on that trip. At least six men had their feet frozen, and two men died in the hospital from pneumonia. They were careless and did not take proper care of themselves. . . .

—Stanley Pearce

*U*p to this point, most things had gone according to plan for Stanley Pearce and Marshall Bond. They had caught one of the first ships headed for Alaska, traveled up and over White Pass, made the five-hundred-mile water journey, and bought a cabin in Dawson City. Now the only thing missing was gold.

In and around Dawson City, gold seemed to be everywhere—in the gambling halls, stores, and saloons and in the surrounding creek beds and hills. In fact, the Klondike region—Eldorado and Bonanza Creeks in particular—contained some of the richest gold deposits ever found on earth.

But finding and extracting gold in large quantities was no small task. Prospectors had to locate a promising piece of land, register a claim with the government, thaw the frozen ground with wood fires, dig a deep shaft, excavate lateral tunnels, haul up buckets of dirt and gravel with a rope-and-pulley windlass, build sluice boxes out of wood, channel water down them, pour in the dirt and gravel, and hope that in the bottom of the boxes would be enough gold nuggets to make it all worthwhile.

Marshall Bond and a few hired workers spent much of the winter and spring of 1898 working the ground this way. Everyone, including Bond, labored long hours—often in the dark—building fires, picking, shoveling, and windlassing. In the evenings, the men had just a few hours of free time, which they often spent talking or playing cards, before going to sleep in the small, crowded cabin.

Louis Bond and Stanley Pearce each made long trips in extremely cold temperatures to follow up on rumors and survey land. In the coming months, Pearce and the Bond brothers would find out if all of their efforts had been worth it—in terms of gold, at least.

Miners thawed the frozen ground with fire, dug down with picks and shovels, and hauled the "pay dirt" up using a rope-and-pulley windlass.

# Marshall Bond Diary

January 14, 1898

Set up the rocker in the cabin & rocked a little but with indifferent results, tho' one bucket yielded $17.00, and one nugget in it $10-.

January 18, 1898

Wick & I rocked all day; we cleaned up $282.50; one nugget weighing $27.00.

Miners slept—and sometimes worked—in dark, cramped cabins.

JANUARY 20, 1898

Left cabin 9:15 a.m. for town. Found Louis at cabin. Pearce had left for "60 Mile" river to do some surveying.

JANUARY 22, 1898

Busy home all morning sawing wood, baking bread, cooking dog food, & gathering things ready to go up to El Dorado tomorrow.

FEBRUARY 3, 1898

Sick in the night & feeling poorly. My left leg is quite painful. I hope it is not from scurvy, & I do not think it is!

FEBRUARY 13, 1898

Rose 5:30 a.m. Started for Dawson 7 a.m. & arrived 10 a.m.—19 miles. Learned that Louis & Pearce had been on a stampede . . . Saw Ex Mayor Wood.

FEBRUARY 19, 1898

46° below 0. Worked at the windlass all the forenoon; and part of the afternoon underground . . . The weather continues getting colder. When the sun comes up in the middle of the day it raises the temperature, but only to drop back again.

FEBRUARY 21, 1898

All day hard at work. The first thing in the a.m. I go underground & help shovel back waste. Then I windlass out the pay dirt.

ON 4th TIER, GOLD HILL. OPPO Nº 5 BONANZA.

After building fires to thaw out the walls of the shaft, miners picked and shoveled to make tunnels. Because the ground all around them was permanently frozen, they did not need to worry about the roofs or walls collapsing.

## FEB. 23RD 1898.

My dearest Mother

I have just returned from a trip of 130 miles on the ice, where I have been doing some surveying and examination of a new discovery on the Sixty Mile River.

I find that in the morning there is a chance to send out mail by a good man—Ex. Mayor Wood of Seattle, so in haste I write you.

My trip was an experience—. I took one man with me and we were gone two weeks. We slept in the tent, we took, every night but two; the thermometer being about 45° below zero the entire time. We pulled on a sled, tent, stove, blankets and provisions and it was pretty hard work.

I have also been off on several 50 and 75 mile trips on foot.... I haven't very much time to write to you Mother, in fact am writing this in town at a young fellow's office which is very cold and full of gossipers....

I am splendidly well really and truly, splendidly well. My nose has been frost-bitten and bears a few scars; but has not as yet spoiled my beauty. I have only borrowed one sheet of paper and envelope so must cut this short....

My plans will be uncertain until May whether I get out or stay; but shall probably get out.

Goodbye and Godbless you Mother.

Your devoted son

Stanley H. Pearce.

# Marshall Bond Diary

February 25, 1898

Wick still troubled with scurvy . . . Gave him some fresh meat, & promised him some evaporated vegetables tomorrow.

March 6, 1898

Everybody worked today but Dan—who spent his time panning in search of rich dirt for rocking and in deluging me with lamentations that I had not the money on hand with which to pay him. I shut him up. . . . The men are terribly bored with Dan's incessant talk of wages.

March 7, 1898

Started for town in afternoon. Before going I discharged Dan whom I found to be an awful liar & mischief maker.

March 9, 1898

Went to Swede Creek where I staked 31 below discovery . . .

March 10, 1898

Left 11:30 for El Dorado. Stopped at 5 below Bonanza & at Skookum to see Bailey & Wick. I was 30 years old to-day.

# THE DENVER REPUBLICAN

DENVER, COLORADO

## LATEST NEWS FROM DAWSON

### Letter of Stanley H. Pearce, "The Republican's" Special Correspondent.

### Situation on the Klondike as It Existed in the Middle of March.

### Midnight Stampede Out of Dawson— Locating Claims by Candle- light—Early Spring.

DAWSON, N. W. T., March 12, 1898.—"The mail is in. The mail is in!" Such was the word which was passed rapidly through the town, up the creek and everywhere where the good tidings could possibly be carried. Everyone seemed to shake off the lethargy and sleepy look which had become chronic.

One of the saloons recently closed was turned into a post-office and the work of sorting and distributing the thousands of letters was commenced by the police. It was three days before any mail could be given out and meanwhile crowds began to gather from the diggings and the excitement was intense.... However, the mail was very old, the very latest letter being written on Nov. 20th. Another lot of mail is expected in a few days when we may hear later news. No newspapers can possibly get in, but the fortunate one who has clippings is in great demand, and it is not an uncommon sight to see a crowd surrounding one in a saloon, while he reads off his news to them....

# GAME OF CLAIM SELLING

We have received vague rumors about the expected rush here in the spring and we all wonder whether there will be such an enormous crowd as reported. What under the sun they will do is more than any of us can tell. Everything in the country is staked and there certainly won't be employment for all hands, as there is not enough for those here already.

Men are busily engaged on schemes to fleece the unsuspecting Cheecakos out of their tenderfoot money, and I am afraid many of them will work.

Perhaps the name Cheecako is not understood by some in Denver, but it is the Saguache name for greenhorn, or newcomer. We "old-timers" are called "sour doughs," as it is supposed to be part of our education to know how to make sour dough bread.

# TYPICAL KLONDIKE STAMPEDE.

A story of the recent stampede to Swede creek is typical of Dawson life. I was awakened at 1 o'clock in the morning by my partner, Bond, who in a mysterious voice told me to "hurry up, dress and come." "Come where," said I. "Don't say a word but come," said he. "How far?" No answer. "Take any grub?" No answer. So I gave it up and came. Slipping a change of socks and moccasins into my knapsack, together with some hard tack, and belting on my hand ax we started in pitch darkness. We reached Tammany dance hall, where there was an unusual bustle and excitement. I was still half asleep and uncertain whether it was a dream or not. Finally we started up the river. There were about 50 in the party, including four or five dance hall girls. It was inky dark and the river trail had been freshly blown over with snow. We have to go up the river and cross it three times. Soon there was trouble. Men and women were off the trail and up to their necks in snow. Finally some one produced a candle and I volunteered to lead the procession, having had experience carrying a candle underground, I therefore had the novel experience of leading a stampede six miles up the Yukon by candle light. Our party of four was one of the first to arrive. We staked by candle light and started home, arriving at Dawson about 9 a.m., having made about 30 miles since 2 o'clock in the morning. Since our staking on Sweede creek, in which I got claim number 20, they have staked as high as No. 750 or about 30 miles above my claim, but I haven't yet found out why we went or what caused that stampede.

Other stampedes are on very much the same order. This, however, is the only midnight stampede on record. Quite a number regretted going to Swede creek on that trip. At least six men had their feet frozen, and two men died in the hospital from pneumonia. They were careless and did not take proper care of themselves. . . .

The days here are getting very long and the sun at last is warm and cheering. Numbers have already been forced to wear smoked glasses for protection to the eyes, as the snowy glare is almost blinding. Fur caps have been put aside and the broad brimmed cowboy hat is the fashionable headgear. Moccasins have been replaced by mucklucks, a water-proof Indian boot, and spring clothes, consisting of overalls and jumper, in my case, are making their appearance. It is not at all unlikely, however, that we will have another change and that 40 below will again make us bundle up in furs.

I hardly think many more letters will reach the states by the ice route after this one, as very few will care to run the risk of starting much later.

I trust that The Republican will do its best to warn Colorado people not to rush in here. Those who come, I can assure you, will never cease to regret the waste of time and money. Yours very truly,

STANLEY H. PEARCE.

"Those who come, I can assure you, will never cease to regret the waste of time and money."

—Stanley Pearce

## MARSHALL BOND DIARY

MARCH 29, 1898

A very warm day. Daylight from about 4:30 a.m. to 8 p.m. Water from melting snow coming in cabin, Walsh & I dug a ditch around it for a drain.

Miners working along a sluice box on claim No. 5 below Bonanza Creek

MARCH 30, 1898

Walsh & I, with help of the two dogs put in the day
hauling sluice lumber from #8 El Dorado. It was hard work.
The last load broke the sled. Ross brought me over a bone
he found in his shaft. I think it is a leg bone of a
mastodon.

---

## DAWSON CITY, N.W.T.
## 10TH APRIL 1898.

Dear Father:—

... The days are becoming quite long & at present from
4 a.m. to 9 p.m. and while at night the thermometer drops to 15
& 20° above zero (and the other night to 4° below zero), in the
day time it runs up to 40° and 50°. ... The snow is melting, and
the trails are getting quite wet. Spring is upon us. Stanley is sitting
... outside, and I am writing with the door open and fine. Nearly
every man wears goggles, but the glare does not seem to affect my
eyes. ... I hope I shall have no more trouble, from now until clean
up. The first of May should see us shovelling into the boxes, and
I hope the clean up will not be disappointing. ... Wickman has
recovered from his scurvy and he and Moore are working for
wages. ... Sometime during the summer I shall start homeward
unless my instincts & judgement tell me it is unwise. ...

Love to all.

Affectionately Yours

Marshall

# Marshall Bond Diary

April 18, 1898

I spent the day picking, shovelling, & night found me thoroughly tired. Men from town say 21 sacks mail has arrived in last two days; that 62,000 people have crossed Chilkoot Pass en route for Yukon country.

May 1, 1898

Clear. 60° above 0. A beautiful day . . . Water in Bonanza & El Dorado very high.

May 4, 1898

Another day of whip-sawing and perhaps the last—maybe in my life. Still I like the work, and should not be sorry to go at it again.

May 11, 1898

Had our sluice boxes up by noon and let water run thro' them . . . In afternoon we began shovelling.

May 16, 1898

Put in the day shovelling in sluice boxes and picking the dump. Riffles show considerable gold.

With water running through the sluice boxes, Bond and his workers shoveled in the dirt and gravel they had dug up from underground. While the lighter sediments were carried

Taken on the porch of their cabin in the warmer days of 1898, this photo shows Stanley Pearce sitting on the steps (far left) and Marshall Bond with his arms crossed (second from right).

away by the water, the heavier pieces, like gold, sank to the bottom. "It was a pretty sight when we shut off the water," Bond recalled. "Often caught and wedged between the poles by their own size, would be glittering nuggets. . . . The nuggets and very coarse gold that could readily be separated by hand were put in a pan, dried and then poured into moosehide sacks."

## Marshall Bond Diary

May 25, 1898

Rose about 10:30. Cleaned gold balance of day. The clean up of yesterday yielded 180 ¾ ozs. . . . I worked till midnight & have turned in. Men stopped 5 a.m.

May 26, 1898

Slept till 5 p.m. To work at 6 p.m. and worked through the night till 5 a.m. It was an unusually tedious and hard night for me. The sun sets in the West about 11 p.m. and rises again nearly where she disappeared at about 1 a.m.

May 27, 1898

To work at 6 p.m. and stopped at 5 a.m. I am feeling poorly & the work seemed unusually hard & long.

May 28, 1898

Stanley arrived about 8 p.m. It was awfully good to see him again, and we put in the night chatting until 5 a.m. when the sluicing stopped.

MAY 29, 1898

A very warm day. Hard work, lack of sleep, and poor grub have about taken the life out of me. . . . Shovelled in until midnight when I was too done up for further work & turned in.

MAY 30, 1898

Stanley & I put in part of afternoon cleaning gold. It is very tedious. Shovelled in in the evening. The water gave out at 1:30 a.m. and I stopped.

---

# # 17 EL DORADO
## 2ND JUNE 1898.

Dear Mother:—

. . . To begin with, I shall start homeward at the earliest opportunity. . . . Have almost finished sluicing Fox's lay. The water is scarce & we have to catch it when others are not using it. When I turned in at 8 a.m. this morning, it was the first time in 28 hours. The men are played out and I have to fairly drag them out of bed, and I do all the cooking, too. . . . Stanley . . . has just left for town to bring us up a little grub, as we are out, and to try and sell the dogs. I told him to ask $500.00. . . . Aleck McDonald, the lucky man of the country, went by last night with four pack horses loaded with 200 lbs of gold each. I have worked out Fox's lay of 44 x 100 ft. and have taken out in round numbers $25,000. . . . In round numbers I shall have $3000, of wh[ich] Louis & Stanley get $1000 each. Deducting Father's 1/3, & expenses out of the country,

& I shall have less than I could have made at home playing marbles or shooting craps. The experience has been a bitter one but an instructive one; and, personally, I can accept the result quite philosophically, but I regret exceedingly the probability of being unable to reimburse Father. . . . As soon as I can get away from here, I shall go to town & commence converting everything into cash, and rustle to dispose of my claims. But my fondest dreams will be realized if I succeed in getting together the $6000 necessary to repay Father. . . . We have been on a diet of beans, rice, bread. . . . I shall be glad to get some fruit & meat. . . . Do not look for me until I turn up, for I don't know when we can get away. The days are very warm now from 40 to 76 in the shade, and there is no night at all. There is considerable scurvy but we are all perfectly well & in no danger of getting it. . . . Stanley will come out about even. . . . I shall have some nice nuggets for you. You cannot possibly imagine how I look forward to going home. The merest trifles one fails to observe in civilization become objects of much thought & adoration here. A bath tub, a chair . . . & all the commonest things are, or seem to be, very grand & great. . . .
But food is the thing the mind constantly dwells on. It appears like a mirage to the senses, ever before the eyes, beautiful to contemplate, but impossible to reach. . . . I shall be as glad to see you again as you will be to see me, but I cant say when that will be, but it will happen as soon as I feel justified in leaving.

Love to all.

Affectionately,

Marshall

> **"We have been on a diet of beans, rice, bread. . . . I shall be glad to get some fruit & meat."**
>
> —Marshall Bond

## Marshall Bond Diary

JUNE 5, 1898

Cloudy 42°. Sluiced whenever we could get water . . . We are now living on beans, stewed apples, and bread. Stanley arrived about 11 p.m.

JUNE 7, 1898

Finished shovelling in at noon. All the dirt but waste is in. Cleaned up in p.m. Am feeling like a wreck.

On June 7, 1898, Stanley Pearce and Marshall Bond scooped their last shovelfuls of gravel into the sluice box. When the water stopped flowing, the inescapable reality became as certain as the rocks in the bottom of the box: they were not going to return home with large sacks of gold. In fact, they were not even going to be able to pay their fathers back for funding the expedition.

Pearce and Bond had done many things right and did find some gold, but it was not enough to make a profit. In the world of prospecting, luck was sometimes just as important as hard work.

On May 29, 1898, an event happened hundreds of miles away that would soon affect Pearce, Bond, and everyone around Dawson City. The ice near Lake Bennett finally broke, and eight hundred boats set sail down the Yukon River that same day. In the coming months, some seven thousand boats would arrive at Dawson City.

Various claims along the same creek had produced more than a million dollars in gold.

On June 9, Stanley Pearce and Marshall Bond finished cleaning their gold and left Eldorado Creek for good. "Our work being ended," Bond wrote, "we took our blankets and gold dust on our backs and started on the seventeen mile hike to Dawson.

"Accompanying us on the trail to Dawson were nine men and four horses laden with a clean up from one of big Aleck McDonald's . . . claims. They probably carried $350,000."

When Pearce and Bond reached Dawson, the streets were crowded with strangers. These were just some of the new stampeders. Thousands more would be arriving in the following weeks, some on whipsawed boats and others on steamships that had taken the all-water route around Alaska and up the Yukon River.

## MARSHALL BOND DIARY

June 10, 1898
The town is becoming crowded with people.

June 11, 1898
Clear. 76°. Beautiful warm day. Went down town about noon . . . Tom O'Brien . . . said several thousand people would be in in the next . . . days.

June 12, 1898
Spent day loafing around watching the new arrivals & the mass of boats wh[ich] line the river bank.

JUNE 24, 1898

Had a little chat with Mrs. Constantine, who is on the Hamilton. Promised to be back in time to say good bye . . . The Hamilton pulled out about 5 p.m. Bade the Constantines good bye, also Col. Bowie, & many others . . .

---

## JULY 6TH, 1898.

Dear Father

Louis Bond suddenly decides to leave on tomorrow's boat. I am writing these few lines for him to mail you on his arrival.

Marshall and I are busy settling up our affairs here and I fear we will be unable to leave before the first of August. It is the hardest place to do anything quickly. The days are twenty four hours long and as everyone sleeps at odd hours, it is difficult to find anyone, particularly as there are from thirty to forty thousand people here now.

I am so anxious to get off, as this place now is simply deadly. We do not wish to sacrifice anything however as long as we are sure of getting out.

Dawson looks more like Coney Island on a holiday, than anything I can imagine. Thousands upon thousands of people wandering aimlessly up and down the water front, without the least idea of what to do or where to go....

You may look for my turning up about the first of September....

Your very affectionate son

Stanley H. Pearce.

In the summer of 1898, disappointed and disoriented stampeders wandered the few streets of downtown Dawson City. Some of them ended up looking for gold, some looked for jobs, and others simply turned around and went back home.

## THE NEWCOMER IN DAWSON.

There are many men in Dawson at the present time who feel keenly disappointed. They have come thousands of miles on a perilous trip, risked life, health and property, spent months of the most arduous labor a man can perform, and at length with expectations raised to the highest pitch have reached the coveted goal only to discover the fact that there is nothing here for them. For these men the NUGGET has a feeling of sincere sympathy, though we are of the opinion that the conditions now existing in and around Dawson are only such as any one might have supposed had he given the matter a few moments of calm and deliberate thought.

*The Klondike Nugget* newspaper,
June 23, 1898

509

While many men found themselves stuck in Dawson, empty-handed, a few returned home with boxes full of gold.

As friends and acquaintances began to leave and thousands of strangers flooded the streets, the intimate town of Dawson that Pearce and Bond had known was fading into history. New restaurants and businesses were opening by the week to meet the new demands of Dawson's booming population. Ships and boats were now importing luxuries like fresh eggs, potatoes, and moose-meat steaks. In a matter of months, Dawson City's population grew from several thousand to more than thirty thousand.

On July 7, Louis Bond boarded the steamship *Alice* and headed down the Yukon River for California. Pearce and Bond would have gladly left Dawson as well, but they still had a cabin to sell and business matters to resolve. In August 1898, more than a year after their adventure began, Marshall Bond (and presumably Stanley Pearce) boarded a boat and started the long journey home.

# AFTER GOLD

These buildings have survived since the
Klondike gold rush days.

# THE RUSH

**I** shall have less than I could have made at home playing marbles or shooting craps.

—Marshall Bond

After the gold rush ended, most stampeders left—and Dawson's streets have been
quiet ever since.

The Klondike gold rush ended as quickly as it began. Word spread that the good claims had been staked, which discouraged another rush of stampeders. Some of the new arrivals stayed in Dawson to work, but many turned around and went back home. Now the stampeders had to decide what to do with the rest of their lives.

Neither Pearce nor Bond returned home to lead quiet lives. Both men continued to seek adventure and search for valuable metals.

## STANLEY PEARCE

Stanley Pearce arrived back in Denver, Colorado, on the morning of September 1, 1898. That day, a journalist from the *Denver Republican* interviewed him in his parents' luxurious mansion on Sherman Avenue. Pearce's story appeared in the newspaper the following day in an article titled "Golden Stories from Klondike."

After the Klondike gold rush, Stanley Pearce moved to Culiacán, Mexico, to develop a gold mine. There, he met and married a Mexican woman named Anita. They had two sons, Albert (Alberto) and Stanley (Stanlito).

In late June 1906, Pearce set off for a business trip and began to feel ill. He thought it was pneumonia, but it turned out that he had developed an infection called erysipelas. Stanley's brother Harold received word that Stanley was sick, and traveled to Mexico to find him. But Stanley's condition had worsened and Harold arrived too late. Stanley Pearce died at the young age of thirty-five.

Harold Pearce wrote the following letter to his mother, informing her about Stanley's death:

## Edwards Hotel, Magdalena, Sonora, Mexico
## July 14th 1906

My Dear Mother

I am making a desperate effort to write you a brief account
of the events which have happened up to the present moment in
connection with our sad mission here.... 

Frank & I left Denver at once on receipt of wire from Latz to
the effect that Stanley had erysipelas, & that Culiacan doctors gave
little hope.... A telegram from Latz informed us that he had died at
Culiacan that morning, Tuesday, July 10th at 9 o'clock.... 

In the morning we were taken to Anita's house to see the
children & the scene there was indescribable. The mother and all
the sisters & other women all shrieking...

With regard to the burial...We feel that you would desire
that dear Stan should be brought back to Denver. The difficulties
however are almost insurmountable.... 

It is very evident that Anita & her family wish to have him here
...There is a nice little undenominational cemetery & yesterday
Frank & I selected an appropriate lot which can be made quite
beautiful in a short time with flowers, shrubs, etc.... 

You would be proud I think to see in what esteem Stanley was
held here, it is very real, and the officers of his company are very
much affected & deplore his loss enormously.... 

I hope you are well in spite of everything.

Your loving son

Harold

Stanlito would drive you mad. You will soon [see] our Stan over
again in this world....

Anita passed away not long after Stanley. Family members brought their two sons, Alberto and Stanlito, back to Denver and eventually to England. The two young men later fought for Great Britain during World War II.

The Pearce family's Christmas photo in Denver, 1903. Stanley and his wife, Anita, sit on the far left with their son Stanlito.

# MARSHALL BOND

When Marshall Bond returned to the family ranch in California, he convinced his father that gold could still be found in the Klondike using hydraulic mining equipment. Bond and his father traveled to London to persuade a mining company to send large equipment to the Klondike, but the deal never materialized. The following year, Bond traveled by ship to the Philippines, hoping to help the United States in the war against Spain. He took care of horses that were transported to the U.S. Cavalry but was never involved in any fighting.

Marshall Bond would continue to seek out adventure for the rest of his life. He searched for gold and silver in Nevada, California, and Mexico. He worked as a newspaper correspondent, a consultant to mining companies, and a stockbroker. He married and had two children. He took frequent camping and canoe trips with friends and family. In 1927, he traveled the length of the African continent, from Egypt to South Africa.

After living a long life and experiencing much, Marshall Bond died from cancer in his midseventies in 1941. One of his sons, Marshall Bond, Jr., wrote a book called *Gold Hunter* about his father's many adventures. One chapter focused on his time in the Klondike.

# JACK LONDON

Like Pearce and Bond, Jack London never found much gold in the Klondike. In fact, he became ill with scurvy and had to return home to California by ship early in the summer of 1898. But once there, London began to write stories based on his experiences during the gold rush. His book *The Call of the Wild,* perhaps his most famous novel, was published in 1903 and launched his literary career. *White Fang* was another of London's best sellers that took place in the Far North.

After the gold rush, Jack London kept in touch with both Bond brothers. London visited the Bond family ranch in Santa Clara, and Marshall Bond visited London at his home in Oakland. In one letter to Marshall Bond, London wrote, "Yes, Buck was based upon your dog at Dawson. And of course Judge Miller's place was Judge Bond's." London also sent a copy of *The Call of the Wild* to Louis Bond, with the handwritten inscription, "Here is the book that never would have [been] written if you had not gone to Klondike in 1897 and taken Buck [Jack] along with you. In fond memory of Sour Dough days, Jack London."

London married twice and had two daughters. In 1916, after a relatively short but prolific literary career, Jack London died at the age of forty at his ranch in California. Nearly a century later, London's writings are still widely read in the United States and around the world.

# THE DOGS: JACK AND PAT

There has been speculation about what happened to Jack and Pat, but no one has ever known for sure. In his letter on June 2, 1898, Marshall Bond wrote that Pearce was headed to Dawson City to try to sell the dogs for $500. Yet according to the book *Gold Hunter*, Louis Bond had tried to bring Jack with him on the S.S. *Alice* but, for some reason, wasn't allowed to do so. He apparently paid for Jack to travel by another boat to Seattle, but when he met the boat, Jack wasn't there. Some evidence suggests that Stanley Pearce sold Pat to a woman who ran a roadhouse and hotel near Bonanza and Eldorado Creeks. So nobody quite knows for sure how or where the dogs lived out the rest of their lives.

Jack, the dog who inspired Jack London's famous canine character, Buck, sits on the left next to Marshall Bond. Pat lounges at Stanley Pearce's feet on the right.

## ALEXANDER McDONALD

At the height of the Klondike gold rush, Alexander McDonald was worth millions of dollars. He owned interests in more than seventy mines and had many men working for him. One of his claims, No. 30 Eldorado, was producing up to $5,000 a day. Yet even though he had gone from rags to riches in a few short years, McDonald wasn't able to stop and enjoy his wealth. He continued buying up more and more claims, many of which turned out to have little gold. Like the majority of the so-called Klondike Kings, he was unable to hold on to his riches for very long. Ten years after the height of the gold rush, Alexander McDonald didn't even have enough money to pay off his debts. In 1909, he had a heart attack and died while chopping wood near his cabin.

Alexander McDonald

## SUCCESS OR FAILURE?

Although the exact figures are unknown, historians do have a general sense of how the stampeders fared over the course of the Klondike gold rush. Out of an estimated one hundred thousand stampeders who set out for the Klondike, only forty thousand ever reached Dawson City. Only half of that number actually worked claims or prospected for gold. The other half didn't even bother trying. And out of the twenty thousand who did work in the goldfields, just three hundred of them found enough gold to be considered rich. This means that less than one-half of 1 percent of all stampeders realized their dreams of finding vast quantities of gold.

Clearly, the disappointment that Pearce and Bond experienced was far more common than the gold-filled sacks of the Klondike Kings. Planning, hard work, money, and perseverance did not guarantee success. Finding gold was not as easy as it had first seemed.

Yet, for many stampeders, an interesting thing happened. Once they returned home and came to terms with their "failure," they realized that the journey had been valuable in other ways. Even though they never found the gold they were looking for, they had pushed themselves to do things they never would have thought possible. In fact, as they grew older, many stampeders looked back with nostalgia on the gold rush and considered it the most exciting time of their lives.

## HIKING THE CHILKOOT TRAIL TODAY

Downtown Dyea is now just an archaeological site, but its neighboring port, Skagway, continues to thrive. Thanks to its history, Skagway is a popular destination for tourists traveling by Alaska State Ferry or cruise ship. Skagway's main street is now full of museums, souvenir shops, restaurants, saloons, and horse-and-buggy rides.

Some visitors pass through Skagway so they can hike the historic Chilkoot Trail. The U.S. National Park Service and Parks Canada work together to maintain the thirty-three-mile trail up and over the Chilkoot Pass. In the summertime, hikers start near the remains of Dyea and end at Lake Bennett. Along the way, they walk through dense forests, across streams, through boulder fields, over snowfields, and down through lake country.

Perhaps the most interesting part of the hike comes near the Chilkoot Pass, where miners left behind gear to lighten their loads. On the way up to the summit, hikers still pass old rusted picks, shovels, tin cans, and teakettles.

Upon arriving at Lake Bennett, the majority of hikers return to Skagway on the historic White Pass & Yukon Route Railroad. The general route of the White Pass Trail, or Dead Horse Trail, can be seen from the train, but it is not a maintained trail like the Chilkoot.

On the Chilkoot Trail, an old, rusted shovel and stovetop with teakettle are just a few reminders of the gold rush days.

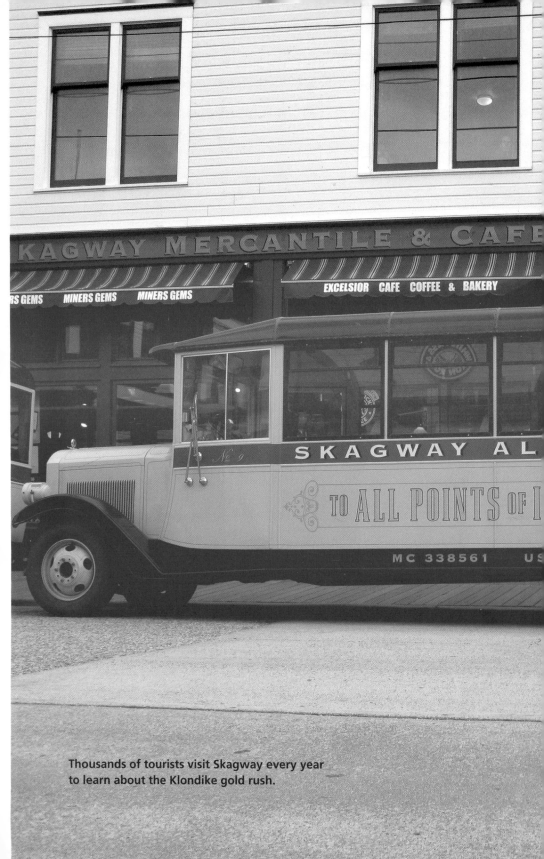

Thousands of tourists visit Skagway every year to learn about the Klondike gold rush.

The White Pass & Yukon Route Railroad from Skagway to Lake Bennett was completed in 1899. Its services would have made the trip much easier for the early stampeders, but it was finished two years too late.

# DAWSON CITY

Dawson City grew from about 1,500 people in the spring of 1897 to more than 30,000 at the height of the gold rush. Tents and temporary structures gave way to sidewalks and large wooden buildings, followed by electricity, running water, telephone service, steam heat, hotels, and restaurants. Despite the development, some modern public services were still missing, such as sewer and sanitation systems. In the summer of 1898, the city was smelly and muddy, and diseases such as typhoid fever and dysentery spread.

Yet almost as quickly as Dawson City's population peaked, it began to decline. Most stampeders, like Pearce and Bond, returned home. Others left town as soon as they heard rumors about new goldfields in Alaska.

From 1896 to 1900, more than $50 million in gold was mined in the Klondike, which is the equivalent of more than $1 billion today. Gradually, individual miners sold their claims to larger mining companies, which continued searching for gold but with more modern technologies, such as high-pressure water cannons and large industrial dredges. To this day, mining companies continue to find and extract gold in the Klondike, though not in the dramatic quantities that were found at the height of the gold rush.

Today, Dawson City is a quiet, peaceful town with just about the same number of residents as it had during the early days of the gold rush. In the summer, thousands of tourists come to learn about the history of the period, stroll the dusty streets, take pictures of old buildings, and visit the famous claim on Bonanza Creek that started it all.

## CASUALTIES OF THE GOLD RUSH

For all of the excitement surrounding the Klondike gold rush, the historic event also produced its share of casualties. Three thousand horses died on the White Pass Trail, and untold numbers of stampeders drowned in the rapids of the Yukon. Numerous lives were also claimed by shipwrecks, avalanches, illnesses, accidents, and murders.

Perhaps less obvious to the outside observer, the gold rush also affected Native people and the land. The Klondike Gold Rush National Historical Park's museum in Seattle notes: "For the Native peoples—including the Tagish, Tutchone, and Tlingit—who had called the region home, the Klondike Gold Rush was

An Indian family at the time of the Klondike gold rush

catastrophic. Miners brought diseases that killed many Native people. Traditional homelands and hunting and fishing grounds were destroyed and traditional food sources vanished. While some found work as packers for stampeders or supplied fire wood for steamboats, they were unaccustomed to a cash economy. Relatively few profited."

As for the effects of the gold rush on the environment, the museum points out: "Initially, Klondike miners dug sediments by hand from stream banks and in underground tunnels. . . . These methods severely damaged the streambeds and streamside habitats. Forests were stripped to supply timber for building and wood for fires to melt sediments.

"In 1897 gold was discovered in the hillsides above the creeks. Soon, entire hillsides were being torn up for gold. Mountains were denuded and wildlife habitat destroyed. Silt and mud from the mining filled creeks, suffocating previously abundant fish populations."

The vast majority of stampeders who poured into Canada's Northwest Territories were American. Escaping their own depressed economy and captivated by gold fever, they were clearly not aware of or concerned about the potentially detrimental effects of their actions on the land, animals, or Native people, who had already been living there for thousands of years.

Today, there are still small-scale mining operations along the famous Bonanza Creek. Deforested areas, scarred hillsides, and large piles of gravel serve as present-day reminders of the Klondike's mining history.

# WHERE DOES
# THE KLONDIKE GOLD RUSH
# FIT INTO HISTORY?

If the Klondike gold rush started today, the event would be completely different. Within minutes of the big discovery, word would spread around the world through the Internet, cell phones, and other modern communication devices. Airplanes would whisk prospectors and supplies directly to the Klondike. Trucks, backhoes, and modern dredges would make the mining process much easier.

But back in 1897–1898, Pearce and Bond had no such options. The only way they could get news to and from the outside world was by handwritten letters. Cell phones, e-mail, and the Internet would not be available for another hundred years. The following timeline puts the Klondike gold rush into perspective by placing it alongside major historical events and developments in communication and transportation.

| 807 | First commercially successful steamboat. |
| --- | --- |
| 849 | Height of the California gold rush. |
| 861 | First transcontinental telegraph line. |
| 861–65 | U.S. Civil War. |
| 869 | Transcontinental railroad completed. |
| 876 | Alexander Graham Bell patents the telephone. |
| 893 | Economic depression strikes. |
| **1897–98** | **Height of the Klondike gold rush.** |
| 898 | Spanish-American War begins. |
| 903 | First powered flight by the Wright brothers. |
| 906 | First vocal radio broadcast. |
| 908 | First mass-produced, practical automobile. |
| 914–18 | World War I. |
| 915 | First transcontinental telephone call. |
| 939–45 | World War II. |
| 940s–50s | Television becomes popular in American homes. |
| 970s | Personal computers become available for purchase. |
| 991 | World Wide Web (WWW) is developed. |
| 990s | Digital cellular phones become widespread. |
| 010s | Use of smart phones and tablet devices grows. |

David Meissner on the Chilkoot Trail

## AUTHOR'S NOTE

I didn't know much about the Klondike gold rush before this project. But one night, while having dinner in New York City, my friend Kim Richardson told me about a bag full of old letters, telegrams, and newspaper articles that a family member had passed down to him. They had been written by his relative, Stanley Pearce, who had been on the front lines of the Klondike gold rush. Kim had found an editor, but they were still looking for a writer to shape these primary documents into a book.

The following week, Kim asked if I wanted to be that writer. His editor happened to be Carolyn P. Yoder, who had published my first magazine article. It seemed as if the stars were aligning. Excited to work with Kim and Carolyn, but still unsure about the topic, I hesitantly said yes.

A short while into the project, I hinted to Kent L. Brown Jr., head of Boyds Mills Press at the time, that if they wanted to send me to the Klondike, I would hike the Chilkoot Trail and do firsthand research. A couple of months later, Kent called and asked if I wanted to go.

I knew right then that this book would be much more authentic. How could I write about the adventures and hardships of the Klondike gold rush while sitting in the comfort of my home in the lower forty-eight states? Although I couldn't travel back in time, I could try to retrace the steps of the stampeders to gain a deeper appreciation for what they faced in the rugged settings of Alaska and the Yukon.

In the summer of 2010, I traveled as far north as Dawson City, in Canada. Admittedly, I did not travel by steamship from Seattle to Skagway. I did not chop down trees, shape the boards into boats, and travel five hundred miles down the Yukon River. Nor did I spend a harsh winter digging for gold.

I reached Dawson City by way of modern-day shortcuts. First, I caught a flight to Seattle, Washington, where I did some research. Then I flew north to Juneau, Alaska, where I caught a six-hour ferry farther north to Skagway, Alaska. After a few days of research in Skagway, I was ready to hike the famous Chilkoot Trail.

On this portion of the trip, I couldn't take any shortcuts. I packed a tent, sleeping bag, and five days of supplies on my back and followed the footsteps of the majority of stampeders. Strewn along the trail were tangible reminders from the gold rush: rusted tin cans, old shovels, a stovetop with a teakettle, horse bones, a sled, and even pieces of leather boots.

The trail itself crosses dirt, mud, gravel, sand, boulders, snow, streams, and bridges. The most stunning feature is the steep, thirty-five-degree ascent up the last part of the Chilkoot Pass. In three miles of hiking, the trail gains nearly 2,500 feet in elevation. The morning we arrived, a steady drizzle was falling, the pass was enshrouded in clouds, and visibility was limited to about 50 feet. My two hiking companions became faint silhouettes in the mist.

We scrambled—sometimes on all fours—over sharp, slippery, and sometimes loose rocks. Near the summit, we crossed a few snowfields before arriving at a small warming hut just after we crossed the border into Canada.

Like Pearce and Bond, I hiked during the summer. I can't imagine hiking the trail in the winter, as many did during the gold rush. There were already enough challenges. On my first day, I missed one simple step over a tree root and badly sprained my left ankle. Within an hour it had swollen to the size of a grapefruit. The next morning, it was deeply bruised. Thanks to ibuprofen and soaking my ankle in cold streams, I was able to continue. One fellow hiker twisted his knee near the summit and had to be flown out by helicopter.

Other parts of my body complained as well. My Achilles tendon hurt, my feet ached, my toes rubbed against my boots, and I had a knot in my neck—all of this despite wearing high-tech hiking boots, an ergonomic backpack, and clothes made of synthetic fabrics that wick away moisture.

Every step of the trail made me appreciate the toughness of these stampeders. I knew that at the end of five days I would enjoy a nice meal, a hot shower, and a comfortable bed. These guys made multiple trips, carried more weight, and were headed toward much more extreme conditions. They didn't have a safety net.

After hiking the trail, I rented a car and drove nine hours north to Dawson City on the most desolate stretch of road I have ever seen. When I pulled into town at 1:30 a.m., an eerie, purple twilight still lingered in the night sky. While in Dawson City, I did my own digging—through old documents, newspapers, and mining claims.

At every stop on my trip, I talked with historians, archivists, librarians, and locals about this book. They told stories, answered questions, and shared their fascination for the legendary gold rush that had shaped their part of the world. The more I learned and experienced, the more intrigued I became. Now if people ask me about the Klondike gold rush, they'd better have a good hour to spare.

It was an unbelievable event in so many ways. Wilderness areas were turned into bustling boomtowns overnight and became deserted ghost towns just as quickly. Man's ingenuity and resourcefulness, fueled by the prospect of gold, had reached new heights. Steam-operated trams were built high up mountain passes. The White Pass & Yukon Route Railroad, although completed too late for most stampeders, was an amazing engineering feat.

The Klondike gold rush provides fascinating insights into the technology, lifestyle, and mindset of the late nineteenth century. I hope this firsthand account of Stanley Pearce and Marshall Bond's shared adventure will help readers step back in time to relive the hardships—and excitement—of the last great gold rush.

—*David Meissner*

# ACKNOWLEDGMENTS

First, thanks to Kim Richardson, for envisioning this book, asking me to be a part of it, and supporting me along the way. His optimism and enthusiasm were contagious. To Carolyn P. Yoder, for her insightful edits and for guiding a young writer through his first trade book. To Kent L. Brown Jr., for taking a chance and funding my own Klondike expedition, an experience I will always remember.

I would also like to thank the many people I met on my trip who went out of their way to share their knowledge about the gold rush: To Karl Gurcke, U.S. National Park Service historian in Skagway, Alaska, for taking the time to answer my many questions and for following up with an incredibly detailed fact check of this manuscript. To Dawne Mitchell, senior interpreter at the Klondike Visitors Association's Jack London Interpretive Museum in Dawson City, for her research assistance and for reviewing this manuscript. How excited I was to finally meet someone who had heard of Pearce and Bond! To Jack London expert Dick North and his wife, Andree, for taking the time to meet and for sharing their knowledge. And thanks to everyone else who facilitated my research along the way: Nicolette Bromberg, visual materials curator at the University of Washington Libraries' Special Collections Division; the research staff at the Seattle Public Library; the research staff at the Yukon Archives in Whitehorse, Canada; David Wymore, park guide at the Klondike Gold Rush National Historical Park–Seattle Unit; and Bruce Hanson, reference librarian at Denver Public Library's Western History and Genealogy Department.

I also want to thank those who helped me along the Chilkoot Trail: To Carol and Ron from Alaska, the couple I met at the trailhead who taught me how to behave in grizzly country and helped me through the ankle sprain. To Kari Rain and the other staff members of the National Park Service and Parks Canada, who answered my many questions and who continue to make the trail accessible to the general public. To the guys at Skagway's Mountain Shop, who helped fit my new pack and piece together my last bits of gear. And to Shannon Reaves, who joined me in Skagway for another memorable writing adventure.

Finally, thanks to the fifth-graders at the Alexander Dawson School in Colorado—Ben, Will, Teo, and Hunter—who read the manuscript and gave me the most authentic feedback of all.

*—DM*

My thanks to my godmother and cousin, the late Ana Carolina Pearce, Stanley's granddaughter, who wanted so much for these letters, telegrams, and articles—which her grandfather wrote from the Klondike more than a century ago—to see the light of day. Stanley's writings were preserved by family members, handed down by each generation, and gifted to me for transcription, editing, and publication. Thanks also to Tom Seavey, who read the manuscript on a visit to London, England, and passed it to Carolyn P. Yoder at Calkins Creek, and to Kent L. Brown Jr. and his inspiring writing workshops.

*—KR*

# BIBLIOGRAPHY*

Adney, Tappan, and E. Le Roy Pelletier. "Map of the Klondike Gold Fields." *Harper's Weekly* and *New York Times*, 1898.

Bond, Marshall. Papers. Yale University, Beinecke Rare Book and Manuscript Library, Western Americana Collection. Includes Bond diary, letters, and two photographs.

Bond, Marshall, Jr. *Gold Hunter: The Adventures of Marshall Bond*. Albuquerque: University of New Mexico Press, 1969.

Bruno, Leonard C. *Science & Technology Firsts*. Detroit: Gale Research, 1997.

*Denver Republican*. "Golden Stories from Klondike." September 2, 1898.

Gurcke, Karl. Interview with author, July 27, 2010.

Hackman, Rebecca. "Klondike Gold Rush: The Perilous Journey North," March 1997. University Libraries, University of Washington. lib.washington.edu/specialcollections/collections/exhibits/klondike (accessed June 10, 2011).

Jack London Interpretive Museum, Dawson City, Yukon, Canada. July 28, 2010.

Klondike Gold Rush National Historical Park, Museum and Visitor Center, Seattle, Washington. July 23, 2010.

Klondike Gold Rush National Historical Park, Museum and Visitor Center, Skagway, Alaska. July 27, 2010.

*The Klondike Gold Rush of 1898: A Resource Guide to "The Last Grand Adventure."* Seattle: Klondike Gold Rush National Historical Park, n.d.

*Klondike Nugget* (Dawson City, YT, Canada). "The Newcomer." Vol. 288. June 23, 1898.

McGrath, Kimberley A., ed. *World of Invention*. 2nd ed. Detroit: Gale Research, 1999.

Mitchell, Dawne. Interview with author, July 28, 2010.

Norris, Frank B. *Legacy of the Gold Rush: An Administrative History of the Klondike Gold Rush National Historical Park*. Anchorage: National Park Service, Alaska System Support Office, 1996.

North, Dick. *Sailor on Snowshoes: Tracking Jack London's Northern Trail*. Madeira Park, BC: Harbour Publishing, 2006.

Pearce, Stanley. "Denver Men on Chilkoot." *Denver Republican*, August 22, 1897.

———. "Denver Men Pushing North." *Denver Republican*, October 9, 1897.

———. "He's Off for the Klondyke." *Denver Republican*, July 28, 1897.

———. "Latest News from Dawson." *Denver Republican*, May 1, 1898, morning ed.

———. "Skaguays Perilous Journey." *Denver Republican*, September 23, 1897.

Richardson, Kim. Interviews with author, December 2009–June 2011.

*Seattle Post-Intelligencer*. "Latest News from the Klondike." July 17, 1897, 9 o'clock ed.

Service, Robert. *The Best of Robert Service*. 1907. Reprint, Mattituck, NY: Rivercity Press, 1976.

Thornton, Thomas F. *Klondike Gold Rush National Historical Park Ethnographic Overview and Assessment*. Final report. Anchorage: National Park Service, Alaska Regional Office, 2004.

*Yukon News*. "Klondike King Went from Rags to Riches, to Rags." MacBride Museum, April 7, 2010. yukon-news.com/opinions/columns/17515/ (accessed June 10, 2011).

# FOR MORE INFORMATION

## Books

Adney, Tappan. *The Klondike Stampede*. Vancouver: UBC Press, 1994. First published 1900 by Harper and Brothers.

Berton, Pierre. *The Klondike Fever: The Life and Death of the Last Great Gold Rush*. New York: Basic Books, 1958.

————. *The Klondike Quest: A Photographic Essay, 1897-1899*. Erin, ON: Boston Mills Press, 2005.

Emmons, George Thorton. *The Tlingit Indians*. Seattle: University of Washington Press, 1991.

Hobbs, Will. *Jason's Gold*. New York: Morrow Junior Books, 1999.

Jones, Charlotte Foltz. *Yukon Gold: The Story of the Klondike Gold Rush*. New York: Holiday House, 1999.

London, Jack. *The Call of the Wild*. New York: Heritage Press, 1960. First published 1903 by Macmillan.

London, Jack. *White Fang*. New York: Puffin Books, 1985. First published 1906 by Macmillan.

Murphy, Claire Rudolf, and Jane G. Haigh. *Children of the Gold Rush*. Portland, OR: Alaska Northwest Books, 2001.

Service, Robert. *The Best of Robert Service*. 1907. Reprint, Mattituck, NY: Rivercity Press, 1976.

# Websites<sup>*</sup>

National Park Service. Klondike Gold Rush National Historical Park, Alaska.
nps.gov/klgo/index.htm

National Park Service. Klondike Gold Rush National Historical Park–Seattle Unit,
Washington.
nps.gov/klse/index.htm

Parks Canada. Chilkoot Trail National Historic Site of Canada.
pc.gc.ca/eng/lhn-nhs/yt/chilkoot/index.aspx

University Libraries, University of Washington. Features the article "Klondike
Gold Rush: The Perilous Journey North" by Rebecca Hackman.
lib.washington.edu/specialcollections/collections/exhibits/klondike

# Video

*City of Gold*. Directed by Colin Low and Wolf Koenig.
Montreal: National Film Board of Canada, 1957.

# PICTURE CREDITS

**Alaska State Library**, Wickersham State Historic Sites Photograph Collection, P277-001-170: 145.

**Dawson City Museum**: 74–75.

**Denver Public Library**: 6 (left), 24–25.

**The Granger Collection, New York**: jacket (main photograph).

**iStockphoto.com/Nnpix**: jacket (nugget inset).

**Library of Congress, Prints and Photographs Division**: LC-USZ62-50194: 33; LC-DIG-ppmsca-08684: 57; LC-DIG-ppmsca-08703: 72.

**David Meissner**: 28–29, 54–55, 68–69, 136–137, 138, 147, 148–149, 150, 153, 156.

Courtesy of the **Pearce family**: 17, 58, 76 (bottom), 141.

Image D-04430 courtesy of **Royal BC Museum, BC Archives**: 38–39.

**University of Washington Libraries, Special Collections**: Seattle Collection, UW 32387: 1; PH Coll 274, Hegg Collection, Hegg 1000: 4, back case cover; PH Coll 722.232, Cooper-Levy Photograph Collection, UW 1617: 12–13; 979.9 L96y, Yukon Gold Fields Collection, UW 32388: 15; PH Coll 482, Asahel Curtis Photo Company Collection, A. Curtis 26440: 22–23; En Route to the Klondike Collection 979.9 L32e, UW 9076: 30; PH Coll 155.75, Edith Feero Larson Photograph Collection, UW 32386: 34; PH Coll 274, Eric A. Hegg Collection, Hegg 181: 42–43; PH Coll 274, Eric A. Hegg Collection, Hegg 3101: 48–49; PH Coll 283, Frank La Roche Collection, La Roche 2132: 51; PH Coll 274, Eric A. Hegg Collection, Hegg 2164: 62–63; PH Coll 283, Frank La Roche Collection, La Roche 2035: 65; PH Coll 274, Eric A. Hegg Collection, Hegg 3190: 80–81; PH Coll 283, Frank La Roche Collection, La Roche 2033: 84–85; PH Coll 274, Eric A. Hegg Collection, Hegg 25A: 96–97; PH Coll 597.9, Klondike: A Manual for Goldseekers Collection,

UW 28771z: 107; PH Coll 274, Eric A. Hegg Collection, Hegg 3089: 108; PH Coll 274, Eric A. Hegg Collection, Hegg 778: 110–111; PH Coll 274, Eric A. Hegg Collection, Hegg 3152: 118–119; PH Coll 274, Eric A. Hegg Collection, Hegg 229: 128–129; 979.905 KL, Semi-Weekly Nugget Newspaper, UW 33310: 133 (top); PH Coll 274, Eric A. Hegg Collection, Hegg 509: 134; PH Coll 274, Eric A. Hegg Collection, NA 2450: 152.

**Vancouver Public Library**, 32866: 10–11, 132.

**Henry Joseph Woodside, Library and Archives Canada**, PA-016223: 104–105.

**Yale Collection of Western Americana, Beinecke Rare Book and Manuscript Library, Yale University**: front case cover, 2–3, 6–7, 76 (top), 89, 90, 122–123, 144.

Original map on pages 8–9 by **Jeffrey L. Ward**.

*To Mom and Dad—*
*for supporting my many paths*
—DM

*To my cousin and godmother, Ana Carolina Pearce,*
*who so much wanted her grandfather's story to be told*
—KR

Text copyright © 2013 by David Meissner and Kim Richardson
All rights reserved

For information about permission to reproduce selections from this book,
please contact permissions@highlights.com.

Calkins Creek
An Imprint of Highlights
815 Church Street
Honesdale, Pennsylvania 18431
Printed in China

ISBN: 978-1-59078-823-3

Library of Congress Control Number: 2013931060

First edition

10 9 8 7 6 5 4 3 2 1

Designed by Barbara Grzeslo
Production by Margaret Mosomillo